JUST FREEDOM

THE NORTON GLOBAL ETHICS SERIES

General Editor: Kwame Anthony Appiah

PUBLISHED:

Climate Matters: Ethics in a Warming World by John Broome

Universal Rights Down to Earth by Richard Ford

Just Business: Multinational Corporations and Human Rights by John Ruggie

Thinking in an Emergency by Elaine Scarry

Can Intervention Work? by Rory Stewart and Gerald Knaus

The Human Right to Health by Jonathan Wolff

FORTHCOMING AUTHORS:

Martha Minow

Sheila Jasanoff

JUST FREEDOM
A Moral Compass
for a Complex World

Philip Pettit

W. W. NORTON & COMPANY

NEW YORK * LONDON

For information about permission to reproduce selections from this book,
write to Permissions, W. W. Norton & Company, Inc.,
500 Fifth Avenue, New York, NY 10110

For information about special discounts for bulk purchases, please contact
W. W. Norton Special Sales at specialsales@wwnorton.com or 800-233-4830

Manufacturing by Courier Westford
Production manager: Anna Oler

ISBN 978-0-393-06397-4

W. W. Norton & Company, Inc.
500 Fifth Avenue, New York, N.Y. 10110
www.wwnorton.com

W. W. Norton & Company Ltd.
Castle House, 75/76 Wells Street, London W1T 3QT

1 2 3 4 5 6 7 8 9 0

For my Ballygar, Canberra, and Vancouver families

CONTENTS

PROLOGUE

In most societies today, on most issues of public concern, we can learn about what is happening from a variety of sources; we can more or less readily inform ourselves about what might have been done and is not done, what is done and might not have been done. Equally, in most contemporary societies we have little difficulty in communicating with one another about what we think is going wrong, using social media to relay complaints about how our public institutions and our public representatives are serving us. This ability to form and exchange judgments on public issues is the bright side of our political life and culture.

The dark side is that it has become harder and harder, in this tumult of data and opinion, to determine which of the complaints made about government are reasonable, which unreasonable. We may be able to tell where our national and international leaders propose to take us but the complexity of the issues and the commotion of politics make it hard to measure the merits of rival initiatives. However transparent the array of options in the public world, the pros and the cons remain obscure. We see the different directions in which our societies may sail but we lack a moral compass to determine which ways are best.

Should our state look after the needy, or leave charity in private hands? Should it set up a system of compulsory medical insurance, or should people be allowed to choose whether to insure themselves or not? Should there be restrictions on private financing of electoral campaigns, or would such a move violate the spirit of an open democracy? Should our central banks and our courts be left in the hands of unelected officials, or should those authorities, like our legislators, have to run the gauntlet of electoral competition? Should each country accept the authority of the United Nations and similar bodies in various domains, or would that be a betrayal of sovereignty on the part of a state? Should rich states be required to help the poor and oppressed, or would that coerce the taxpayers of those states into an involuntary form of charity?

Unless we are ostriches, questions like these are bound to confront us in our everyday lives. But how are we to make up our minds on any such issue, whether as ordinary citizens, public officials, or would-be activists? Once we have sorted out the facts of the case to our satisfaction, how are we to determine what is right and what is wrong? The ideal solution would be to find a compelling reference point for making those judgments, in particular one that came from beyond the adversarial scramble of day-to-day politics. Such a reference point would provide a moral compass to guide us in a principled way through the thicket of public issues. Combined with factual assumptions about the background to those issues, it would help us to see where we ought to take our stand.

To be plausible, any reference point would have to be an ecumenical value—or set of values—that people on all sides of politics could recognize as relevant, assuming that they are ready to treat others as equals with themselves. It would not have to be a value to which all are ready to give unique authority in their thinking about politics, but it should at least be a value that all can recognize as a plausible candidate for such a directive role. It should be a value whose sponsors, when they defend its claims, might reasonably expect to get a hearing in all quarters.

Given the variety in contemporary conceptions of the good life, it may seem that a moral compass of this ecumenical kind is a pipe dream. But despair would be premature. I make a case in this book for building a moral compass around the notion of freedom, an ecumenical value whose political relevance no one is likely to contest. Interpreted in the fashion associated with the age-old ideal of the republic, this simple value has the potential to give us a unifying and revealing perspective on the many issues raised by our complex contemporary world. Recast in its original republican mold, freedom can provide a compelling viewpoint from which to gauge issues of political right and wrong. It is sufficient in itself to ground a nuanced, persuasive philosophy of public life. So, at any rate, I hope to persuade you.

THE MEANING OF FREEDOM

In late 1879, the Royal Theater in Copenhagen staged the inaugural production of Henrik Ibsen's play *A Doll's House*. The play took Denmark and Europe by storm and established Ibsen's enduring reputation as one of the world's great dramatists. Like any good piece of theater it raises many important questions, but I find it fascinating for the question it raises about the meaning of freedom in particular.

The main figures in Ibsen's play are Torvald, a relatively young and successful banker, and his wife, Nora. Under nineteenth-century law Torvald has enormous power over how his wife can act, but he dotes on her and denies her nothing—nothing, at least, within the accepted parameters of life as a banker's wife. True, he bans the macaroons for which she has a particular taste. But even that denial is not much of a restriction, since she can hide the macaroons in her skirts. When it comes to the ordinary doings of everyday life, then, Nora has carte blanche. She has all the latitude that a woman in late nineteenth-century Europe could have wished for.

Nora enjoys many benefits that anyone might envy. But does she enjoy freedom? In particular, does she enjoy freedom in her relationship with Torvald? His hands-off treatment means that he does not interfere with her, as political philosophers say. He does not put any prohibitions or penalties in the way of her choices, nor does he manipulate or deceive her in her exercise of those choices. But is this enough to allow us to think of Nora as a free agent? If freedom consists in noninterference, as many philosophers hold, we must say that it is.[1] But I suspect that like me, you will balk at this judgment. You will think that Nora lives under Torvald's thumb. She is the doll in a doll's house, not a free woman.

If you agree about this, then you should be ready to endorse the conception of freedom driving this book. Your freedom as a person requires more than just being let alone, just benefiting from noninterference; it requires richer assets than any that Nora enjoys. To be a free person you must have the capacity to make certain central choices—choices about what religion to practice, whether to speak your mind, who to associate with, and so on—without having to seek the permission of another. You must be able to exercise such basic or fundamental liberties, as they are usually called, without having to answer to any master or *dominus* in your life.

Freedom in this sense requires the absence not just of interference, but of the subjection to another that was known at the time of the Roman republic as *dominatio* or domination (Lovett 2010, Appendix I). As we shall see more fully in Chapter 1, it was in that republic, and in the many later republics that modeled themselves on Rome, that the ideal of freedom as non-domination was most sharply articulated and most enthusiastically embraced. The freedom of the person was equated in those regimes with the freedom available to the fully incorporated, adequately empowered citizen.

The absence of interference that Nora enjoys is not enough for freedom in this sense, since it only comes about by Torvald's grace and favor. In order to enjoy freedom you must have the ability to avoid interference even if others take against you, and this is precisely what Nora lacks. If Torvald took against her and withdrew his goodwill, then she would no longer enjoy noninterference at his hands. Thus, as things stand, she is indebted to him for the latitude of choice that she enjoys. She is subject to his will, by virtue of his legal and cultural power, and it is only her good fortune, not the status of being a free woman, that explains why she escapes his intrusion in her life.

What Nora needs, if she is to be truly free, is not just the absence of interference, then, but the absence of domination: that is, the absence of subjection to the will of others, in particular Torvald's will. We shall have much more to say about domination in later chapters, but the general idea should be clear. To enjoy such non-domination in her life Nora would have to enjoy protection against anyone else's capacity, should their will tend that way, to interfere in the exercise of her basic liberties. She would have to be given adequate safeguards against any arbitrary interference in her choices—any interference that might be practiced without her invitation or permission.

Nora's predicament ought to be familiar. Think of what it is to be in a position where you may or may not suffer ill-treatment, depending on the whim of another, be it a teacher or boss or bank manager, an insurance agent or a counter clerk, a police officer or immigration official or prison warden. Think of what it is to have no physical or legal recourse against such an uncontrolled or arbitrary presence in your life, to be under the power of that other, depending on the goodwill of the person to avoid suffering some loss or harm. Such dependence amounts to the same unfreedom that Nora endures. If you happen to be treated with indulgence and goodwill, as Nora is, then you will of course be a lot better off than if you incur the malice of the other. But even if you escape ill-treatment, you can only congratulate yourself on your good fortune, not on your freedom.

If this conception of freedom as non-domination resonates with you and if you think that such freedom is valuable for all, then that is bound to give you a critical perspective on contemporary society. You must acknowledge the value of social and political arrangements that were lacking in Nora's milieu, and are often lacking also in our own. We pride ourselves on how much freedom we have won in the modern era, at least in many of our societies, but when judged by the ideal of freedom as non-domination even the most welcoming of polities fall short. A society in which people enjoy freedom as non-domination would require a republic of mutual empowerment and mutual respect that our different countries currently approximate in only a patchwork and partial measure.

This takes me to the theme of the book. Freedom as non-domination is a challenging ideal that offers a picture of the sort of progress that we should hope for, and look for, in the social and political organization of our world. And, more important, it is almost unique among challenging ideals in providing a plausible, unifying yardstick for measuring the level of social and political progress in any society.

None of us can be indifferent about the assessment of national and international arrangements, as they raise issues that we all have to confront as observers or activists or officials. Thus we all need a criterion for determining which complaints about existing arrangements are fair, which unfair, which proposals for change ought to be embraced, and which dismissed as underinformed or overly idealistic. The proposal of this book is that the ideal of freedom as non-domination fits the bill. It enables us to chart where and how far our different communities, and the world as a whole, fall short of what justice requires. It can serve us like a global positioning device, a GPS, enabling us to find our way around the complex political issues with which the twenty-first-century world confronts us.

JUSTICE IS FREEDOM, FREEDOM JUSTICE

In considering what would make a society just, we confront issues in three categories: social justice, political justice, and international justice. I maintain that we can treat all of these issues as questions, at bottom, of how best to promote the enjoyment of freedom as non-domination.

Consider first some issues of social justice: that is, issues in the relations between the citizens of any one society. How should a government organize the shared legal and economic lives of its citizens? Should it let people make their own fortunes and lives within an established, unyielding framework? Or should it protect the less fortunate against poverty and destitution, against the lack of medical care, and against the absence of legal representation in a criminal trial? Should it provide legal and social recourse against domestic abuse or, more generally, against the sort of dependency exemplified by Nora? And in that case, should it also provide protection for those who are dependent on the goodwill of an employer or creditor, a union or a corporation, in much the way that Nora is dependent on Torvald?

The standard approach to such questions invokes our intuitions about what justice means and about what it demands in the context of a particular society. Those intuitions are often vague and conflicting, however, with one person being convinced that justice supports a rugged individualism, another that it requires a radically redistributive state. The freedom ideal suggests a different, more sharply focused approach. This is, to let the requirements of social justice be determined by an investigation into which social arrangements would best promote people's enjoyment of freedom as non-domination.

The legal and economic order of a society determines the extent to which the relationships people form with one another do or do not allow some people to dominate others in the domain of presumptively personal, basic choices. And so, to anticipate later argument, the freedom ideal naturally implies that various forms of destitution and dependency are objectionable and unjust. The injustice of such maladies consists in the fact that each affliction is certain or likely to put the affected parties at the mercy of others. Unless the poor and the ill are adequately secured, for example, they will be in a position where they depend on the goodwill of the more powerful to maintain their capacity to live as they wish: their capacity to exercise their personal choices according to their own preferences. If you are impoverished—if you lack the resources to function adequately in your society (Sen 1985; Pettit 1993; Nussbaum 2006)—then you are likely to live in fear of how the rich and powerful will treat you, should you speak your mind frankly or exercise no caution about whom you associate with. This being so, it becomes plausible to think that we can determine what social justice requires by working out the legal and economic order of a society that would enable you and others to live in freedom: to be able to conduct your personal lives without others having the power to interfere in what you choose.

Freedom as non-domination is not the only good in life, of course. But it is a gateway good, as we might put it: a good whose realization promises to bring the realization of other goods in its train. If we look after freedom as non-domination in the context of domestic legislation and government, guarding against people's dependency on others in areas of properly personal choice, then we will also have to look after goods such as social, medical, and judicial security, domestic and workplace respect, and, more generally, a functioning legal and economic order. If we pay the admission price for freedom, then we will have paid enough to ensure access to those other more specific values as well.

This suggests that in matters of social justice, freedom need be the only guiding good: it can operate as a regulative ideal for policy-making and a yardstick of justified criticism and protest. But freedom as non-domination serves as a touchstone not only for social justice. The two other principal domains of concern in politics—political justice and international justice—also stand to benefit from the guidance it provides.

Take some issues of political justice: that is, justice in the relations between citizens and the government that rules their lives. Should voting be the only means whereby citizens can influence the selection and performance of elected represen- tatives? Should lobbying be allowed? Should private financ- ing of electoral candidates be permitted? Should election be confined to members of the legislature and perhaps the head of the executive, or be extended also to judges and other officials? And if judges and other authorities—auditors, stat- isticians, ombudsmen, central bankers—are appointed rather than elected, what sorts of briefs and constraints ought to be imposed on them?

We can usefully think about how to resolve these knotty questions by reflecting on what people's freedom as non- domination requires in their relation to government. Govern- ment inevitably involves interference in the lives of citizens, whether via legislation, punishment, or taxation. Our ideal sug- gests that this interference need not be dominating, however— and need not be inherently inimical to freedom—so long as the people affected by the interference share equally in controlling the form that it takes. Let state interference be guided equally by the citizenry and it will not reflect an alien power or will in their lives. Thus the ideal argues for a regime under which the interference of government is exercised on terms laid down by the people and not at the unlimited discretion of those in power. Such a regime would count in a strict and demanding sense as a democracy. It would live up to the Greek etymology of the word, providing the people, or *demos*, with power, or *kratos*, in relation to their government.

In looking at issues of political justice, then, we do not have to fall back on our varied, often vague intuitions about the demands of justice in this area. We merely have to consider what is required if people are to be un-dominated by those in power, even as those in power interfere in their lives. We can deal with these and many other questions in the course of asking ourselves about the institutions, electoral and non-electoral, that are needed if people are to share equally in controlling the way that government treats any one of their number.

The same general line applies in international justice: that is, justice in the relations between the different peoples of the earth. Should the different peoples of the world enjoy certain sovereign liberties regardless of the will of others? Should their sovereignty in this regard protect them not just against other states, but also against multinational organizations and international agencies? And should such sovereignty be something that different peoples are required to defend themselves, or should it be protected in international law and administration? Going to more specific matters, what duties, if any, do wealthier peoples have to aid the impoverished in other, ill-performing societies? And what duties, if any, do they have to protect other peoples against domestically oppressive governments?

As with questions of social and political justice, these questions of international justice can be usefully treated as issues of freedom as non-domination. They sound out some of the requirements that an international order must satisfy if it is to provide properly for the independence or sovereignty of each society: its capacity to make its own way, on its own terms. Dangers include the problems raised by domestic impoverishment and domestic oppression—hence the issues of international aid and protection—but they also include the danger to the independence of a people from exposure to the interference—military, economic, or diplomatic—of a more powerful state, or exposure to the interference of a multinational corporation. We need to examine what is required of the international order if the planet's different peoples are each to enjoy freedom as non-domination—not just freedom as noninterference—in relation to one another's states and in relation to other non-state bodies. We need to know what it should be like if it is to ensure the rich sovereignty of peoples held out by the freedom ideal.

I have been arguing that the conception of freedom as non-domination allows us to see all issues of justice as issues, ultimately, of what freedom demands: what it demands in our social relations with one another, in our political relations to our government, and in the relations between the different societies on earth. Integrating these diverse issues under the rubric of freedom serves a simplifying purpose, offering a thread that can lead us through what may otherwise seem like a dense and impenetrable jungle of problems.

But the exercise can serve a unifying as well as a simplifying purpose. The ideal of freedom is a candidate criterion of political assessment according to almost all schools of political thought. Thus, building an overall political philosophy—a philosophy of social, democratic, and international justice—on the foundation of freedom as non-domination has natural ecumenical attractions. It would leave room for differences that are driven by different readings of the background facts or by different weightings of the rival requirements of freedom. But it would guard against political divisions becoming as nonnegotiable as differences of intuition and taste.

There are many interpretations of freedom, of course, but as Nora's example illustrates, linking freedom with non-domination, and not just with noninterference, has powerful intuitive attractions. And this construal also has a long heritage. As suggested already, the ideal goes back to the Roman republic and, as we shall see, it remained the commanding vision of freedom down to the time when it became the rallying theme in the republican revolutions in America and France. The ideal of freedom as non-domination offers tested and solid ground on which to build, albeit ground neglected in contemporary thought—and ground that we need to consolidate as a basis for pursuing contemporary argument.

John Keats wrote, with some license, that the sum of all required knowledge—all we know and all we need to know—is contained in the line "Beauty is truth, truth beauty." The refrain I mean to strike in this book, to put it in somewhat embarrassing parallel, is "Justice is freedom, freedom justice." This slogan catches the idea that we need not despair at the various and complex challenges of justice in social, democratic, and international contexts. The ideal of freedom as non-domination can mark out a clear and attractive pathway. It can provide a moral compass for holding our path in a world that is complex to the point of being downright bewildering.

A MORAL COMPASS

The compass, I should stress, is a moral compass. It is not meant to furnish specific guidance on the institutions that figure in our different social and democratic societies, and our shared international world. Any empirical guidance that it offers on the character of such institutions is only a secondary, incidental benefit. What it primarily aims to provide is a means by which to steer in thinking about the right and the wrong of those institutions, and the right and wrong of the initiatives that they allow political authorities to take.

If you are like me, you will often be appalled by how things are developing in the political world but find yourself unsure about how best to critique the situation or, should you happen to be in government, how best to adjust policy. You may rail, for example, at how great an impact moneyed interests have on government, or at how governments treat illegal immigrants, or at the intrusiveness of government in one or another area of the economy. But still you may wonder about the best grounds on which to question the state's performance in these areas, or even if it ought to be questioned in the first place. If this book serves its purpose, it should help to resolve this sort of uncertainty. It argues that in each such case the ideal of liberty provides the required yardstick. All you have to do is ask whether things can be better arranged for promoting freedom as non-domination among relevant parties.

I do not expect, of course, that it will be immediately clear what the yardstick of freedom requires. That is why I have written a book, not an article. The book is designed, first, to spell out the requirements of freedom as non-domination and, second, to sketch the social, democratic, and international institutions for which they would argue, looking at how far those institutions plausibly count as just. In part 1, I begin with the long history of freedom, which emphasizes the link with non-domination, and I go on to elaborate an overall view of freedom's demands that preserves that linkage. In part 2, I turn to more concrete issues, arguing that the satisfaction of those demands is likely, under plausible empirical assumptions, to support clear and appealing images of what social justice, political justice, and international justice require.

Rather than speaking in a cumbersome way of social, political, and international justice in this investigation, I shall speak more simply of the value of justice in the first case, democracy in the second, and sovereignty—that is, the sovereignty of peoples—in the third. Justice in the narrower sense—that is, social justice—is the virtue of a national or domestic framework in which people's relationships with one another are subject to a just social order: one, intuitively, that gives people the resources and protections of equally free citizens. Democracy is the virtue of a national framework in which people's relationships with the state that imposes that social order are subject to a just political order: one, intuitively, that lets people share equally in control of the state and enjoy equal freedom as its masters. And sovereignty is the virtue of an international framework in which the relationships of different peoples with one another are subject to a just global order: one, intuitively, that allows each society to govern itself effectively as a sovereign and free community.

A handful of slogans sums up my claims about these connections between freedom and the more specific values of justice, democracy, and sovereignty. Let people enjoy freedom as non-domination in their relationships with one another and they will enjoy a genuine form of justice. Let people enjoy freedom as non-domination in their relationships with their state and they will enjoy a demanding variety of democracy. And let the different peoples of the world enjoy freedom as non-domination in their relationships with one another, and with other multinational and international bodies, and they will each enjoy a proper form of sovereignty.

Some readers will be more interested in the policy proposals in these three areas than in the historical and philosophical roots of the ideal of freedom employed in defending the proposals. With the help of the themes rehearsed in this prologue, and the overview of the book provided in the appendix, it ought to be possible for such readers to go straight to the policy discussion in part 2 of the book. This approach would involve exploring the implications of the ideal of freedom as non-domination without first focusing on the argument in support of the ideal, which is presented in part 1.

TESTING FOR JUSTICE,
DEMOCRACY, AND SOVEREIGNTY

Freedom as non-domination is bound to come in degrees. In any context, it may be more or less well protected against relevant individuals or bodies. And it may be protected across a wider or narrower range of choices. So what level of freedom must people enjoy in order to count as having access to justice, democracy, and sovereignty? I invoke three user-friendly tests in order to answer the question. The three tests, respectively, are the eyeball test, the tough luck test, and the straight talk test.

The eyeball test requires that people should be so resourced and protected in the basic choices of life—for short, the basic liberties—that they can look others in the eye without reason for fear or deference of the kind that a power of interference might inspire. When you enjoy social, medical, and judicial security, and benefit from a suitable legal and economic order, you do not depend for your security on the indulgence and condescension of others. You can walk tall and assume the status of an equal with the most powerful in the land. At least, you can do so provided that you do not count under local criteria as excessively timid or paranoid.

The tough luck test requires that the government should support and protect its people on the basis of such equally shared control that if a collective decision goes against you, then you have reason to view this as tough luck, even by the most demanding local criteria, and not as the sign of a malign will working against you or your kind. If government decides to allow a prison to be built near your backyard, for example, then it does so on the basis of processes and principles of decision-making that you join with others in endorsing; it is not the product of a coalition of hostile interests out to get you or your neighbors. Thus you can feel that the adverse decision about the prison was just bad luck, at least if you do not count under local criteria as timid or paranoid; you can think of the decision as an unfortunate setback on a par with a bout of illness.

Finally, the straight talk test requires that the peoples of the world each have such resources and protections in dealing with other states and other global bodies that the contributions of their representatives in international debate and diplomacy can reasonably be construed at face value. They are contributions made in public exchanges where the parties each command respect; none has reason to speak in the presumptuous tones of the master and none in the mealymouthed tones of the servant. Thus, if a people's representatives assume a different posture, say by deferring to the spokespersons for another state, for an international agency, or for a multinational corporation, then by contemporary criteria they can be accused of timidity or paranoia.

Why do I put such an emphasis on local and contemporary criteria in formulating these three tests? Because there is no plausible, species-wide criterion for determining when enough is enough in providing for justice, democracy, or sovereignty. The stroller who walks briskly and securely down a contemporary street might freeze in terror at the prospect of navigating a medieval city, which would cause no apprehension in a local of the time. Similarly, the job-seeker who worries about the prospects of employment in one of our developed countries would be utterly shocked at the insecurity of employment in even the freest cities of eighteenth-century Europe or America. It would be silly to have tests of justice, democracy, or sovereignty that are insensitive to such salient cultural variations.

The argument presented in support of the ideals associated with my three tests is inevitably sketchy, and this book should be taken neither as a theoretical treatise nor as a practical manifesto. My hope is that it may alert others to a way of thinking about politics that is modest in the base from which it begins, starting out as it does from the requirements of freedom alone, and yet substantive in the principles and policies that it supports for organizing our lives together. The chapters on justice, democracy, and sovereignty all end with a section on "the bottom line," where I have tried to bring out the substantive character of the recommendations supported by the discussion. In each case this is an attempt to compare the approach with alternatives and to illustrate the sorts of commitments that it would enjoin.

Many of those who are broadly persuaded by the first part of the book, acknowledging the claims of freedom as non-domination, will not agree with some of the recommendations made on justice, democracy, and sovereignty. This is to be expected. Those recommendations depend not just on philosophical reflection about the history, meaning, and importance of freedom, but also on the nature of the empirical assumptions made about institutional feasibility and, of course, on the quality of imagination brought to bear in considering institutional designs. The approach is not a blueprint for setting the world to rights but a research program for developing the normative theory of justice and for elaborating the demands of justice in our social, democratic, and international institutions. This book is an invitation to join in pursuing this program, not an account of an already settled doctrine or ideology.

PART 1

The Idea of Freedom

Chapter 1

THE PAST AND PRESENT
OF FREEDOM

WHEN ARE YOU FREE?

A common metaphor suggests that you are free insofar as you are given free rein in your choices. If you have all the leeway or latitude you could wish for, if you enjoy carte blanche in determining how to act, then by this suggestion you enjoy freedom in the fullest measure. The phrase "free rein" is drawn from horse-riding. When a rider lets the reins hang loose, the horse enjoys free rein: it can go in whatever direction it wishes. When you are given free rein, so the metaphor suggests, you too can take whatever path you choose: you are under no one else's operative control.

A little reflection suggests that free rein may fail to realize the best we might expect of freedom, both for the horse and for the human. When I give a horse free rein, I do not use the reins to direct it, nor do I let the reins hang loose because the horse happens to be going in the direction I prefer; not having any preference in the matter of direction, I let the horse go as it will.[2]

But while giving the horse its head in this sense, I remain in the saddle, ready to pull on the reins should my wishes change. I do not exercise operative control over the horse, then, but I do enjoy potential or reserve control. And as that holds in the literal case, so it holds also in the metaphorical. When I give you free rein, I refrain from exercising operative control, but I still enjoy the reserve counterpart of that control. I may not pull on the reins but I do remain in the saddle.

Consider the case that we discussed in the prologue. In *A Doll's House*, Nora is given exactly what free rein requires, being free of any operative control on Torvald's part. But Nora is not free in the sense of non-domination, since she remains subject to her husband's reserve control. Let Torvald have a change of mind, or let Nora begin to act in an unwelcome way, and he will use the reins at his disposal to impose his will.

But we do not have to go to the theater to find examples of such reserve control or reserve power. The homeless who depend on charity to get a bed for the night, the seriously ill who depend for medical treatment on the pro bono services of a doctor or hospital, the employees who hang on the whim of employers for keeping their jobs: all such people are in a position like Nora's. Because they are lucky they are able to enjoy shelter, work, and sustenance—and are even able to exercise the basic liberties that presuppose such goods—but this does not give them freedom as non-domination. It provides them only with free rein.

It is significant that free rein began to be invoked as a metaphor for freedom in the nineteenth century, and not before. Up to that time, the dominant way of thinking about freedom emphasized that to be free in any range of choice you had to escape not just the operative control of others but even their reserve control. In this earlier way of thinking, the free horse was the horse unharnessed, not the horse that happened to be given its head. The republican opponent of monarchy Richard Rumbold must have had that image in mind when he stood on the scaffold in Edinburgh in 1685, waiting to be hanged for treason against the Crown. Insisting on his continued allegiance to a republic, he declared, "I never could believe that Providence had sent a few men into the world, ready booted and spurred to ride, and millions ready saddled and bridled to be ridden."

On the older way of thinking that Rumbold invoked, freedom in a range of choices requires avoiding any form of control by others. The control to be avoided may be the operative form of control in which others are disposed to impose restrictions as that becomes necessary for the satisfaction of their wishes. Or it may be the reserve form of control that consists in having a power to assume such an operative role. If I can limit your discretion in the choice of option or can impose my terms on how you choose, I have a degree of reserve control over what you do. Your capacity to choose this or that option is going to depend on the state of my will as to whether you should choose as you wish. If I want you to have discretion, then you will choose as you wish; if I cease to want this, you will not. But in either case you are going to remain subject to my will and in that sense unfree. I will remain at all times in the saddle.

In this way of thinking, you could count as a free person or citizen only to the extent that you are your own master—you are *sui juris*, in the expression from Roman law—in a range of choices that were already known in Rumbold's time as the fundamental or basic liberties (Lilburne 1646). These choices, available in principle to any citizen, were taken to include choices over what religion to practice, what party to espouse, what associations to join, as well as where to reside, how to earn your living, and so on. We shall have much to say about them in the third chapter.

If, like Rumbold, you embrace freedom in the traditional sense and reject any control on the part of others, you aspire to the position of the independent person who has no master or *dominus* in their life. Freedom in this view consists in being able to make your choices without any need to seek another's permission. That way of articulating freedom goes back to at least the Romans, who were familiar with the institution whereby a master or *dominus* held power over his slaves. They argued that to live *in potestate domini*, in the power of a master, was enough in itself to make you unfree. Having a gentle master might be a boon in other ways, but it did not give you liberty.

To be a *liber*—a freeman, in the established English translation—as distinct from a slave was to be secure against the power of any master in the domain of the basic liberties; it was to be safeguarded against the *dominatio* or domination of others in the exercise of discretion within that sphere. The thing that gave you such security—the thing that gave you freedom as non-domination—was having the status of a *civis* or citizen, someone adequately and equally guarded by the law. In particular, it was having the status of a citizen who is guarded by a law that is itself controlled by the citizenry, not something imposed by a super-master such as a king or an aristocracy. In this Roman way of thinking, as one writer puts it, "full *libertas* is coterminous with *civitas*" (Wirzubski 1968, 3); being free and being a citizen are essentially equivalent.

What should we call a political philosophy that grounds itself in this ideal of freedom as non-domination? Because it has its origins in republican Rome, and because it has always been associated with the rejection of monarchy—or at least, of a monarchy unbound by a constitution—the most appropriate term is probably "republicanism" or perhaps "civic republicanism" (Honohan 2002). But republicanism in this sense amounts to much more than a mere rejection of monarchy. And despite its influence in the founding of the United States, it is quite distinct from the American political party that claims the republican name.[3]

The republicanism outlined here is, inevitably, a philosophy addressed to today's concerns and it reflects the contributions of a number of contemporary authors.[4] But since it attempts to build on an idea with a long history, it has inescapable connections with past republican thinking. I shall be referring at various points in the book to earlier republican authors, and in this chapter I offer a quick sketch of the development and eventual disappearance of the tradition.[5] In the next two chapters I shall put history in the background and look at how to rework the rich republican conception of freedom into a contemporary ideal.

If you prefer your philosophy neat, unlaced by historical antecedents, you may wish to go straight to those chapters, perhaps relying on the overview of the argument in the appendix to get a sense of what you missed. My own view is that the history provides a vivid context for the understanding of the philosophical argument and that it helps to show that the viewpoint developed in this book is not some newfangled way of thinking but belongs squarely within a well-aired, well-tested tradition.

THE ROMAN REPUBLIC

It was a Greek who spent many years in Rome, first as a hostage and then as a willing visitor, who offered the initial sketch of what Romans came to think of as their distinctive philosophy of government. In the middle of the second century BCE, Polybius wrote an extended history of Rome that highlighted what he saw as the glory of the Roman republic and the benefits it provided for its citizens: in effect, the permanent male residents of the city who were not held as anyone's slaves. In this account, Rome gave citizens freedom in relation to the power or *dominium* of private masters insofar as the law afforded equal and adequate protection for each. And Rome gave citizens freedom in relation to the law itself—to the public power or *imperium* at the origin of law—insofar as it ensured that the law reflected the shared wishes of the citizenry.

The Roman republican tradition's insistence on equal legal status for free citizens required that no citizen be given greater legal rights than others. In other words, it sought to protect people in their horizontal relations with one another. But this equal legal status called at the same time for equality in exercising control over the law. There should be no monarch or elite who could tailor the law to their own particular will or taste. Such equality would protect people in their vertical relations with the state, or the government that runs the state, ensuring that they have equal control in the shaping of the law. A republic, as it came to be conceptualized, is nothing more and nothing less than a community organized around these ideas of equality before and equality over the law.

Polybius was particularly effusive about the control over the shaping of law that the Roman constitution gave the citizenry. The power to form, enact, and administer Roman law was put in the hands of mutually checking, popularly representative bodies and officials. This power materialized in an arrangement Polybius called a mixed constitution. The arrangement was constitutional insofar as public, impartial law governed it; and it was mixed insofar as it gave power to all sectors of society.

Laws were made in Rome by governmental bodies in which all citizens could take part, on the basis of proposals from officials. And while the officials who proposed such laws were members of a senatorial elite, they had to be popularly elected to office and they were subject to a variety of checks. Thus their term of appointment was typically just one year. At each level of authority there were always two or more officials elected—at the very top of government, for example, two Consuls. And any decrees or policies could always be vetoed by one of the ten tribunes elected to represent the interests of the plebeians; these were generally the poorer classes among the citizenry.

Needless to say, republican Rome never lived up to the ideal of a republic where citizens were secure against both horizontal or private domination and public or vertical domination. Differences in wealth and influence made many citizens the clients or dependents of others, and the constitution generally operated for the benefit of elites. But whatever its faults in practice, the abstract idea of a republic of equally free citizens—a republic of freemen—became lodged in European consciousness as a result of the work of Polybius and the Roman republican thinkers he inspired. These included lawyers and philosophers like Marcus Tullius Cicero and historians like Titus Livius or, as we know him today, Livy.

MEDIEVAL AND RENAISSANCE REPUBLICANISM

The republican ideal that guided Rome for over five centuries faded to the status of a ghostly presence in the period of the Roman Empire—this began with the reign of Augustus about the beginning of the common era—and in the Dark Ages that followed the collapse of that empire about 500 CE. But the ideal resumed life and influence six hundred years later in the high Middle Ages, as the burghers of the independent trading cities of northern Italy looked for a philosophy to shape and express what they enjoyed as free citizens, thanks to their independence of prince or Pope. In cities like Venice and Florence, Pisa and Perugia, public institutions came to be organized on something akin to the Roman pattern. And as classical literature became better known in the course of the Renaissance, the model of republican Rome was routinely invoked as a paradigm of what these cities had achieved or were in sight of achieving.

Although he is now better known for the scandalous amoralism of *The Prince,* the Florentine diplomat Niccolò Machiavelli was particularly influential in the development of republican ideas through his *Discourses on Livy,* published at the height of the Renaissance in 1531. Like earlier Roman authors, he hailed civic freedom—the freedom as non-domination enjoyed by the citizens of a republic—as the signature ideal, and argued that it could only be achieved under a mixed constitution of the kind that Polybius had praised. He argued in particular for a constitution that allowed ordinary citizens to contest government in the way the Roman plebeians had continually contested the proposals and decisions of their rulers, whether in popular elections or demonstrations, via their tribunes or in the courts.

After Machiavelli, it became clear that there are three broad claims associated with republicanism. The first claim is that the ideal of freedom as non-domination should be paramount in social and political life. The second is that the promotion of that ideal requires some version of the mixed constitution. And the third is that the preservation of that constitution requires ordinary citizens to be able and willing to contest public power—to be able and willing to assert their free status in relation to any authorities. Freedom as non-domination is the ultimate end. The mixed constitution is a necessary means for achieving that end. And a contestatory citizenry is a necessary means for keeping the mixed constitution in place.

In the centuries after the Renaissance, the neo-Roman framework defined by these three claims underpinned the political self-understanding of northern European countries that resisted or overthrew absolute monarchs. These included the Polish republic of the nobles in the sixteenth and seventeenth centuries, the seventeenth- and eighteenth-century Dutch republic, and the English republic of the 1640s and 1650s. Across Europe, republicanism became the dominant political philosophy of reformers and revolutionaries. And, unsurprisingly, it became the despised target of criticism for absolutist writers who argued that the peace of the commonwealth required a single sovereign with more or less absolute power.

The most prominent absolutists were Jean Bodin in sixteenth-century France and Thomas Hobbes in seventeenth-century England. Each worried that a republican philosophy that supported a mixed constitution and favored a citizenry willing to contest those in power would stoke civil dissension and rebellion. Living in the wake of the Protestant Reformation, at a time of continued religious division, both men saw reason to be concerned about giving the people a republican variety of influence and control. They worried in particular that a state without a single, dominant head to guide it would be a many-headed monstrosity at continual war with itself.

SEVENTEENTH- AND EIGHTEENTH-CENTURY REPUBLICANISM

While the English republic was the shortest-lived of the regimes that embraced republican ideas—it lasted from 1649 to 1660—it had the widest influence and the deepest impact. The republican ideas that emerged among defenders such as James Harrington,

John Milton, and Algernon Sidney became a staple of political thought in eighteenth-century Britain and in its American colonies, albeit usually adapted to make room for a constitutional monarchy. They permeated the influential work of the Baron de Montesquieu, *The Spirit of the Laws*, published in the 1730s; he wrote this under the spur of enthusiasm for what was then described as the British constitution. And the ideas were the more or less common property of a host of combatants in early eighteenth-century Britain, among them the Whig establishment, their Tory opposition, and the radical Whigs who delivered a constant sting in the side to every establishment. These radical Whigs included English critics of the home government, such as the authors of the critiques gathered together as *Cato's Letters* (Trenchard and Gordon 1971). Most significantly, their ranks included the American colonists who invoked republican ideas in criticism of subjection to the Parliament in London as well as their British supporters, such as the mathematician Richard Price and the chemist Joseph Priestley.[6]

The trigger for American outrage was the imposition of the Stamp Act in 1765, which required the colonies to use stamped paper for various official documents and to pay a tax to the British for the use of that paper. The uproar it caused led to the repeal of the act just a year later, but in issuing that repeal, Parliament announced a Declaratory Act designed to chasten the colonists. In this act, Parliament claimed as "of right" to have "full power and authority to make laws and statutes" to bind the Americans. It asserted, in other words, that it could interfere as it wished in the lives of its American subjects. From the perspective of the Americans, it meant that they had little or no control over how government treated them and could no longer regard themselves as freemen in relation to the law.

The Americans lacked electoral representation and the control it afforded, as did many of the British themselves: hence the slogan "No taxation without representation." They also lacked the control provided by a constitution under which those who pass laws and impose taxes are themselves subject to the provisions they introduce. It was the absence of even this basic form of control that Joseph Priestley (1993, 140), fastened on. "Q. What *is* the great grievance that those people complain of? A. It is their being taxed by the parliament of Great Britain, the members of which are so far from taxing themselves, that they ease themselves at the same time."

The tax imposed by the British Parliament may not have been particularly heavy, as indeed the tax imposed in the Stamp Act had not been heavy. But the point for Priestley, as for the Americans, was not the size of the tax but the parliament's claim to power. As he went on to explain: "by the same power, by which the people of England can compel them to *pay one penny*, they may compel them to pay the *last penny* they have. There will be nothing but arbitrary imposition on the one side, and humble petition on the other." The same point was emphasized by Priestley's friend Richard Price (1991, 77–78). Commenting that individuals under the power of masters "cannot be denominated free, however equitably and kindly they may be treated," he argued that the same lesson applied to societies like Great Britain and its colonies: "This is strictly true of communities as well as of individuals."

It may seem unusual to lay such stress on the role of republican thought in the American War of Independence without commenting on the French Revolution. While republican ideas played an important part in the uprising of 1789, and in later French thought, they did so in the untraditional shape that Jean-Jacques Rousseau had given them in *The Social Contract*, published in 1762.[7] In that work, Rousseau had endorsed the republican idea of freedom as non-domination, lamenting the dependency of any human being on the will of others. But, because he followed Bodin and Hobbes in rejecting the idea of the mixed constitution, he was led to defend a political arrangement that broke sharply with received republican ideas (Spitz 1995; Pettit 2013b).

Rousseau developed the idea that the best defense of the independence of individuals in relation to one another comes, paradoxically, from their each accepting dependence on the community as a whole, in particular their dependence on the sovereign assembly of the people. While every citizen should "be perfectly independent of all the others," he says, this is only possible insofar as each is "excessively dependent on the City" (Rousseau 1997, II.12.3). Contrasting the sovereignty that a collective people would enjoy with the sovereignty possessed by a private lord or master, he put forward a consciously outrageous slogan: "each, by giving himself to all, gives himself to no one" (I.6.8). To those in the older republican tradition—for example, to Machiavelli or to Harrington—Rousseau's vision would have appeared to celebrate a form of dependency on the will of the corporate whole—in effect, the will of the majority—at odds with a vision of freedom as non-domination.

The Rousseauvian version of republican thought might be better described as communitarian in character. It casts the community, embodied in the citizen assembly, as a defender of people's freedom against others. And it suggests that that community is not in itself a danger to freedom, at least when the assembly operates with a view to the good of the whole. Since it imposes only the general will, so the idea goes, the community cannot dominate those who share in that will. This communitarian aspect led Rousseauvian enthusiasts in the nineteenth century to abandon the idea of freedom as non-domination and replace it with the idea that the free citizen is someone who enjoys the right or experience of participating in communal decision-making. With that development, Rousseau's project lost all connection with its republican origins.[8]

Rousseauvian republicanism did not sound the death knell for the neo-Roman or Italian–Atlantic republicanism with which we are concerned here. Rather, as we must now see, it was the rise in Britain of a new way of thinking—associated with utilitarian and liberal developments—that achieved that result. This brought about the eclipse of republicanism in two distinct stages and ushered in a way of thinking, still predominant today, in which freedom as non-domination is replaced by the much less demanding ideal of freedom as noninterference.

THE ECLIPSE OF REPUBLICANISM: PHASE 1

The American War of Independence represented the high point of influence for Italian–Atlantic republicanism. By a curious irony, however, it was at this very time that another way of thinking about freedom emerged to displace republican ideas. Under this conception, freedom in any choice requires just the absence of restriction or interference, not the absence of domination. You can enjoy freedom, in other words, just by enjoying free rein; it does not matter that another party sits in the saddle, retaining reserve control over how you choose. The new approach was first developed among British opponents of the American cause, being used by them to make a case in favor of the colonialism practiced by the mother country.[9]

John Lind, a paid apologist for the British government, made that colonial case quite openly in a popular pamphlet, "Three Letters to Dr Price" (1776), in which he sought to rebut Richard

Price's arguments on behalf of the Americans. He argued that freedom requires only noninterference; it is "nothing more or less than the absence of coercion," whether coercion of the body or the will (16). British law certainly interferes in the lives of the Americans, he says, imposing compliance and levying taxes, since "all laws are coercive" (24). But the law also interferes in the lives of the British themselves, he argues, so that the Americans can have no particular complaint about being deprived of their liberty by British law (114). According to the conception of freedom that he espouses, their liberty is no more affected by the imposition of law than the liberty of the British themselves; it is irrelevant that the law is imposed on the Americans from without and on the British from within.[10]

Where does Lind get his new conception of freedom from? He acknowledges in a footnote that he owes it to "a very worthy and ingenious friend" (17). That friend turns out to be the founder of Utilitarian thought, Jeremy Bentham, who had already begun to use the conception in developing a view of law and the state that would later make him famous. He had written a letter to Lind a short while before the appearance of the pamphlet, explaining that the view of freedom as nothing more nor less than "the absence of restraint" was "the cornerstone of my system" and came of "a kind of discovery I had made" (Long 1977, 54).

At the time of Lind's pamphlet, Bentham was himself opposed to the American cause, and he did not object to Lind's use of his purportedly novel conception of freedom.[11] But Bentham was moved by a larger concern than the desire to defend British colonialism. He was a social reformer who believed that the concern of the state should not be limited, as it had been limited in almost all previous philosophies, the republican included, to propertied, mainstream males; everything should be ordered toward "the greatest happiness of the greatest number." And so he held that the state should be concerned with the freedom or liberty of all its subjects, not just the freedom of an elite citizenry. But in arguing for this point of view, he cast freedom in his own words as consisting in nothing more than "the absence of restraint." He consciously rejected the stronger claim that freedom might require the absence of a restraining power on the part of others.

Why did Bentham advance this weaker ideal of freedom, one in which people are not made unfree by living under the dominating power of another, only by suffering actual interference? The reason may have been a failure of his reformist nerve. Were Bentham to have called for universal freedom as non-domination, then he would have had to advocate the transformation of family law, under which a husband had power over his wife, and master–servant law, under which an employer had power over his employees. These may well have been challenges at which he balked. He could look for universal freedom as noninterference without having to embrace such radicalism, for the wife of a kind husband, or the servant of a kind master, can be free in his thinner sense. They may each have to live under another's power of interference, as existing law required, but if the husband or master is kind then they do not have to endure actual interference and do not suffer unfreedom as Bentham's newly formulated ideal represents it.

Perhaps it was with such thoughts in mind that a close associate of Bentham's, William Paley (2002), described the older idea of freedom as too radical to be taken seriously. He admits in a work published in 1785 that freedom as non-domination, which "places liberty in security," accords well with "common discourse" (313). But then he insists, paradoxically, that in contrast to the new conception of freedom as noninterference, it demands too much. It is one of those ideals of "civil freedom," he says, that are "unattainable in experience, inflame expectations that can never be gratified, and disturb the public content with complaints, which no wisdom or benevolence of government can remove" (315). How could Paley have thought that the established conception of freedom was too radical and revolutionary, given his recognition of its deep roots in history? Like Bentham, he was a reformer engaged in arguing that freedom should be a more or less universal ideal. I suspect that as he began to think about what freedom as non-domination *for all* would require, the traditional conception began to seem too radical and the novel conception looked like the only feasible and appealing ideal.

THE ECLIPSE OF REPUBLICANISM: PHASE 2

The republican way of thinking did not merely undergo a late-eighteenth-century challenge to its account of the meaning of freedom, with the ideal of noninterference displacing that of non-domination. Soon afterward it also confronted a challenge to its account of the range of choices in which people ought to enjoy freedom if they are to count as free persons.

If freedom is interpreted in a rich and demanding way, as it is in the republican way of thinking, then it follows that people cannot expect to enjoy freedom as persons or citizens—or not, at least, equal freedom—except within a common range of choices that are important in everyone's personal life. These are the choices that were known in seventeenth-century republicanism as the fundamental or basic liberties (Lilburne 1646). They encompassed that variety of choices, considered important for any citizen, that people could each enjoy at one and the same time: choices over what to think and say, what religion or party to espouse, what occupation to pursue, and so on.

If freedom is interpreted in an austere, less demanding manner, however, as it is in the conception of freedom as noninterference, then things look very different. There is no obvious reason in this case to think that promoting freedom, even promoting more or less equal freedom, should be limited to catering for the privileged range of choice associated with republican citizenship. Let freedom mean just the absence of constraint, as it meant for Bentham and his followers, and an increase in freedom will come with an increase in the absence of any constraints.[12] Moreover, let freedom mean just the absence of constraint, and equality in freedom between you and me may come of an absence of constraint, not in the same sphere of action, but across quite different ranges of choice. You may be free insofar as you enjoy latitude and leeway in your preferred, bohemian pattern of life, I may be free— indeed equally free—insofar as I enjoy latitude and leeway in the more puritanical mode of existence that answers to my taste.

The different attitudes to the range of choices in which you might expect to enjoy freedom showed up in the early nineteenth century in the different interpretations given to what was described as freedom of contract. In the republican view, freedom of contract naturally meant the freedom to enter or refuse to enter into a role or relationship whose terms were already well established in law and custom: the freedom to enjoy the liberties associated with that position. If you were free to marry, that meant you were free to decide whether or not to take on the duties and rights of a husband or wife, as they were commonly understood, not free to negotiate about those duties and rights and then to make a decision. If you were free to enter a trade or profession, that meant that you were free to decide on whether or not to become apprenticed to a master under traditional terms that neither you nor the master could alter. And if you were free to travel on an oceangoing ship, that meant you were free to decide on whether or not to assume the rights and obligations that custom and law gave you as a passenger. But with the new understanding of freedom to hand, freedom of contract began to be interpreted in a much more radical fashion. It came to mean the freedom not just to enter into established roles or relationships, but to negotiate the terms of any such post or association (Atiyah 1979). And with the rise of this new understanding of free contract, it became second nature to think that you were free to the extent that you did not have to act under any constraints other than those you had negotiated contractually.

This shift of conceptual perspective fit snugly with the social changes that were transforming the world in the early nineteenth century. Industrial and commercial developments shattered the mold of traditional occupations and relationships. They created new opportunities for entrepreneurs in the economic and financial world, new conditions of employment for those working in the factories and mines that entrepreneurs established, and new living and housing arrangements for the tens of thousands of peasants who poured into the ever-growing cities in search of work and survival. These changes undermined the traditional assumption that different roles and relationships had nonnegotiable contours and that freedom could only consist in access—ideally, equal access—to established possibilities.

In these circumstances a new group of thinkers, known to us as classical liberals, took advantage of the construal of freedom as the absence of constraint or interference and argued that the promotion of freedom, even equal freedom, was perfectly consistent with this transformation of traditional society. Invoking freedom of contract, they celebrated and championed greater and greater latitude in the contractual arrangements that people could establish in the workplace, in the market, and in cross-border commerce. They called for giving people carte blanche in setting the terms on which industrialists and other employers could hire workers, entrepreneurs could establish their enterprises as incorporated companies, mining companies could operate their mines, and providers could offer their services. Thus, they even rejected the idea that oceangoing passengers should have predetermined rights that went with paying for passage, and campaigned for passengers to be able to negotiate away such rights—and put their health and lives at serious risk—in return for lower fares (MacDonagh 1980).

With the advent of such ideas, the cause of freedom took on a very different complexion. Classical liberals argued that the ideal of freedom called unambiguously for removing all constraints and letting people, powerful and powerless alike, negotiate the terms on which they entered relationships or provided services for one another. This line of argument suggested in particular that the coercive, un-negotiated interference of the state should be minimized. Classical liberals called for more and more deregulation—for freeing up the economy and, by implication, society at large. Where government had been cast by eighteenth-century republicans as the great champion of freedom, providing a system of law under which citizens could be secured in the enjoyment of their basic liberties and could count therefore as free citizens and persons, it now began to look like the villain of the piece: the source of regulations that did more to hamper than to help the cause of freedom. Classical liberals would have cheered Ronald Reagan's claim nearly two hundred years later that government is the problem, not the solution.

Those attached to the republican way of thinking about freedom, by contrast with those who embraced the new libertarianism, were repelled by the working conditions that prevailed in the early to mid-nineteenth century. In their view, the mines and factories of the world's rapidly industrializing societies were little better than slave camps. Men, women, and indeed children were driven for want of a better alternative into accepting conditions that clearly denied them an undominated status in relation to their betters. They might have signed up freely for the employment offered, which was the point always emphasized by classical liberals, but the contract they entered allowed employers unrestrained discretion in how they treated their workers. Employees had no alternative but to accept such discretion; if they did not, they could be fired at will and, as often happened, find that they were blackballed among other potential bosses.

Republicans who took these conditions to jeopardize freedom as non-domination rejected the freedom of contract hailed by classical liberals and denounced the new arrangements on the grounds that they turned industrial workers into what they described as "wages-slaves" (Sandel 1996). Thomas Jefferson sounded the complaint with characteristic brio, opposing the introduction of industry to the new United States. "And with the laborers of England generally, does not the moral coercion of want subject their will as despotically to that of their employer, as the physical constraint does the soldier, the seaman, or the slave?" (Katz 2003, 13).

But this republican response to the new industrial world faded in the course of a few decades, as the idea of wage slavery was taken up by other groups and used for other purposes. In America it was appropriated by defenders of chattel slavery, who used it to argue that the slave plantations of the American South were no worse than the industrial factories of the North

(Foner 1970). And in Europe, it became the catch-cry of social-
ist movements that were more focused on concrete, signature
policies—for example, nationalizing the means of production—
than on the requirements of an abstract commitment to freedom. In the newly emerging struggle between workers and
employers, then, the ideal of freedom became the property of
the classical liberal school alone and largely disappeared from
the lexicon of the opposition.

There is one further development to register, however, in this
brief history of freedom in the nineteenth century. Classical liberalism was challenged in the later century by modern liberalism, as it was called at the time (Gaus 1983). This is personified
by John Stuart Mill. While broadly faithful to the thought of
his Utilitarian father, James, John Stuart Mill was greatly influenced by the German Romantic movement which had stressed,
in words that Mill (2001, 54) quoted from Wilhelm von Hum-
boldt, that the end or purpose of the human being is "the high-
est and most harmonious development of his powers." This led
him to maintain that every person should have that range of
free choice that would allow for "the free development of indi-
viduality." (53).

Mill believed, in the spirit of Romanticism, that the freedoms needed for self-development would differ from individual to individual. Rather than list the choices that ought to be
established in law, which would have furthered a republican
conception of freedom as a status to be accorded to individuals,
he insisted more abstractly on the need for law to give each person maximum scope for the realization of his or her potential.
The individual, he said, is "accountable to society" only for
"such actions as may be prejudicial to the interests of others,"
and where sanctions do not do more harm than good, these
actions may be subjected to legal sanction (86). Otherwise,

however, individuals should have rights against their state, and rights against their fellows, to be let alone in whatever they decide to do.

At times, Mill shows signs of thinking in terms of freedom as non-domination, as when he argues against "the almost despotic power of husbands" and suggests that giving women the same legally protected rights as men would ensure the "complete removal of the evil" (96). But generally he equates freedom with noninterference, and where the demands of freedom as noninterference are not enough to spur a call to remedy what he saw as social ills, he invokes the broader ideal of utility or happiness. When he confronts the ills associated with the low wages of workers, for example—say, in Adam Smith's (1976, 351–52) example, the ill of not being able to afford a pair of leather shoes—he never suggests that those low wages undermine freedom: say, as Smith thought, by exposing the person to shame, thereby restricting social and other options. Instead, he urges the rectification of those evils on the independent ground that it would advance the workers' utility or welfare (Mill 2010, Bk 2). The notion that an increase in wages might mean an increase in freedom goes unaddressed.

REPUBLICANISM, LIBERALISM, AND LIBERTARIANISM

There is a fairly sharp contrast between republicanism and either the classical or the modern forms of liberalism just described. Unlike the republican approach, both forms of liberalism construe freedom as noninterference, equating it with being let alone. But like republicanism, they both hold up freedom as a paramount or central ideal in political life. Classical liberalism makes freedom as noninterference into the single guiding value of political life, whereas modern liberalism tends to have a somewhat wider focus; Mill, for example, recognizes other requirements, apart from freedom, as essential for human welfare or happiness.

There are many contemporary varieties of liberal thought. All share in common the notion that freedom is equivalent to noninterference, thus preserving a contrast with the republican school. But they vary in two important ways: first, in whether they take freedom to be the only value, thus tending toward right-wing policies, or as a value to be balanced by a typically left-wing concern for material and other kinds of equality; and second, in whether they lay as much stress on constitutional forms—the rule of law, the separation of powers, and entrenched legal rights—as they do on the freedom or other values that allegedly support such forms.[13]

Thus, liberal schools of thinking divide into three main categories. Standard, right-wing libertarians assert that freedom as noninterference is the only value and have little or nothing to say about constitutional forms. Minority, left-wing libertarians hold that freedom as noninterference is important but so is material equality, in particular, equality in the common ownership of the earth (Vallentyne and Steiner 2000). And constitutional liberals, as we may call them (Laborde 2013), hold that freedom and equality are both important but so too are constitutional arrangements such as the rule of law, the separation of powers, and entrenched legal rights.[14]

Constitutional liberalism is what is usually described as liberalism in North America. Its recent, outstanding spokespersons include John Rawls (1971; 1993) and Ronald Dworkin (1986; 2000). It has republican roots insofar as those invoked as its principal heroes are the seventeenth-century English thinker

John Locke and the eighteenth-century German philosopher Immanuel Kant, both of whom were closely associated with the republican tradition. This association shows up in their view of freedom, particularly in their view of freedom as requiring the security provided by law, not as something that law reduces, as Bentham and others argued.[15] While continuing to think of freedom as noninterference, or so I interpret them, thinkers like Rawls and Dworkin often strike themes that are close to the republican outlook that I will present here.[16]

Because of the linkage of constitutional liberalism with republican thought, it does not offer as good a foil to republicanism as nineteenth-century liberalism or, in today's terms, libertarianism. The contrast between libertarian and republican thought runs very deep indeed and is well worth emphasizing.

According to libertarians, freedom, which consists in being let alone, would be perfectly available even if there were no other people on earth; freedom in this sense used to be regularly described as natural liberty. In the libertarian way of thinking, the laws and norms that protect you in society are mere instruments for getting you as close as possible to the condition of natural liberty. When properly composed, they provide the best that social life allows in unhampered latitude of choice. According to republicans, by contrast, freedom presupposes society and consists in being secured against the power of others in that society to intrude on your basic liberties; freedom in this sense was traditionally described as civic, as distinct from natural, liberty. In this rival way of thinking, the laws and norms of your society promote your freedom in the sense of providing the security that it requires. They are not causal means or instruments that bring the ideal of freedom closer; to the extent that they provide the required security, they are means that constitute the very freedom they serve.

According to the republican picture, the laws and norms that establish you as a free person provide you with freedom in the way that antibodies in your blood provide you with immunity. Once you have antibodies against a certain disease, from that moment on you enjoy immunity from it. The antibodies don't have to do anything causal to make you immune; they don't bring about your immunity, as they might bring about a distinct effect. They make you immune just by being there; they constitute your immunity just by providing you with protection against potential invasion. In the same way, the laws and norms that give you the status of a free person—provided they are effective—do not bring about your freedom, as they might bring about a distinct causal effect. They make you free in a constitutive manner, just by being there, insofar as they provide you with protection against potential interference in the sphere of your basic liberties. From the moment they are in place, they incorporate you in a protective and empowering force field and establish you in the enjoyment of your freedom.

Both libertarian and republican schools of thought take freedom as a value and seek to identify the laws and norms that can best advance it.[17] But they start from very different presumptions about what freedom essentially consists in, with one construing it as natural liberty—the freedom of the heath—and the other taking it to consist in civic liberty—the freedom of the city.

The difference in presumptions has a distinct impact on policy preference, as we shall see later. Laws and norms often involve interference with the people on whom they are imposed, being supported by the threat of jail or fine or other sanction. And so libertarians—in particular, standard libertarians, for whom freedom as noninterference is the only value—take the view that so far as freedom is concerned, law and government

should always be kept to a minimum. Republicans are not unin-
hibited enthusiasts for law, recognizing as they do that law often
hinders more than it helps. But they do not view the recourse to
laws and norms with an equally cold eye. For them government
is an essential means of promoting freedom and while it may be
misused, as the means to any goal may be misused, it cannot be
marginalized or dispensed with.

THE PROJECT

I said earlier that republicanism became a ghostly presence in
imperial Rome, and throughout the Dark Ages, before being
revived in the northern Italian cities during the high Middle
Ages. The same may be said of republicanism in the period
since the rise of nineteenth-century liberalism. True, constitutional liberals generally argue for a variant on the mixed constitution defended by earlier republicans, and they all support
something approaching a contestatory role for citizens; like
republicans, they oppose absolutist government. But like their
libertarian fellows, even constitutional liberals overlook the
fact that power in itself—that is, the power of imposing an alien
will—is inimical to freedom, and that freedom against such
power requires securing people in the choices that define them
as equally incorporated citizens.

The philosophy that I sketch in this book tries to retrieve
and rework the republican insights that have been eclipsed over
the past couple of centuries.[18] Liberalism made a great stride
forward in recognizing that the citizenry of any state should
be inclusive, not restricted to mainstream, propertied males,
and any revived version of republicanism must incorporate this
development. But it must not balk, as Bentham and Paley may

have balked, at arguing that this inclusive citizenry should enjoy freedom as non-domination, not merely freedom as noninterference, and should enjoy it in all the basic choices of life. It must be prepared to explore the ideal to its last implications.[19]

That is what I try to do in the remainder of the book, reworking the lessons of the republican notion of freedom for how to organize society. In the two remaining chapters of part 1, I lay the groundwork for that investigation, articulating and defending a conception of freedom that remains true to the republican tradition. In chapter 2, I look at how the ideal of freedom in choice, taken at its best, supports deep requirements of the kind associated with freedom as non-domination. And in chapter 3, I explore the breadth or range of choices over which people should enjoy such deep freedom if they are to count as free persons. In part 2, I examine the policy implications of such a renewed republicanism in the domains of justice, democracy, and the sovereignty of peoples.

The character of Nora in Ibsen's *A Doll's House* offers a vivid example of someone who enjoys freedom as noninterference—indeed, freedom as noninterference across a relatively wide range of choice—but who lacks freedom as non-domination. It may be useful to keep Nora in mind as we look at the depth and breadth of republican freedom. In chapter 2, we shall be looking at the deep level of protection that Nora must have against her husband, and against others in general, if she is to count as free. And in chapter 3, we shall be exploring the broad range of choice across which freedom requires that she be protected at that deep level.

Chapter 2

FREEDOM WITH DEPTH

I introduced the case of Nora to illustrate what it is for someone to enjoy noninterference without enjoying non-domination. To illustrate this same possibility, the Romans relied on the example of a slave who is lucky enough to enjoy his master's benevolence, charming enough to win the master's indulgence, or cunning enough to escape the master's attentions. The slave who congratulates himself on how free his good fortune or sharp wit enables him to be is a figure of fun in Roman comedies (Skinner 1998, 40–41). As any Roman audience would have been aware, such a slave is self-deceived. You are not free if you have a master, however good or gullible that master may be. In the words of Algernon Sidney (1990, 441), a seventeenth-century republican thinker, "he is a slave who serves the best and gentlest man in the world, as well as he who serves the worst."

In the republican way of thinking, both in the time of Rome and later, freedom does not come cheap. It requires a form of security associated with citizenship and incorporation within a protective law. Thus the Romans themselves held that even a slave without a master—a *servus sine domino*—is not a *liber* or freeman; only the *civis* or citizen can lay claim to that protected status (Wirszubski 1968).[20]

In this chapter, I explore what exactly is required for someone to enjoy freedom of the sort that escapes our fictional Nora and our fortunate slave. I concentrate on how you might enjoy freedom in a particular choice, or particular type of choice, explicating the requirements that must be fulfilled in any choice that is going to count incontrovertibly as free. The republican tradition was focused mainly on what it is to enjoy freedom as a person or citizen, as we have seen, not just freedom in a particular choice or type of choice, but I will take up that topic in the next chapter, when I ask about the breadth or range of choice that a free person requires.

The discussion in this chapter is more abstract and philosophical than anything that follows and it may require more patience than an author is generally entitled to expect in readers. What it tries to do is to establish the core republican point, that to be free in a choice it is not enough to get what you want. You must be able to get what you want regardless of what it is that you want. And you must be able to get what you want regardless of what others want you to get. Your freedom in that sense must have depth. I go on to argue in the next chapter that if you are to be free as a person you must have that deep freedom, not just in this or that choice, but in all those types of choices that are traditionally cast as the basic or fundamental liberties. You must have a broad as well as a deep form of freedom.

A FORMULA FOR FREEDOM IN CHOICE

What exactly is a choice? I take it to be nothing more nor less than a set of options or alternatives that are within your control or, as we say, up to you.[21] Thus, you may have a choice between only two alternatives, perhaps between raising your left hand or raising your right hand. Or you may have the distinct choice between three alternatives: raising your left hand, raising your right hand, or raising neither. The options involved in a choice may involve your immediate body, as in these last examples, or reach out into the world, as in the choice between sending an email, making a telephone call, or mailing a letter. These options reach out into the world in the sense that they are available to you not just by virtue of your innate capacity, as with the choice between raising your left or right hand, but by virtue of the technology and infrastructure of the surrounding society.

What, then, does it mean to say that you enjoy a free choice between certain options? Take a choice Nora might face: between going to the theater with a female friend or staying at home with Torvald. Or take a choice that you might face: between sending a message via letter, telephone, or email. What conditions would ensure the enjoyment of a free choice between such options? Or better, what conditions might make for a greater probability or degree of freedom in the exercise of the choice?

I propose the following formula as an articulation of the required conditions.

You enjoy freedom of choice between certain options to the extent that:
  1. you have the room and the resources to enact the option you prefer,
  2. whatever your own preference over those options, and
  3. whatever the preference of any other as to how you should choose.

The best way to make sense of this account of freedom of choice will be to defend each of the three clauses in turn. In the sections that follow, I try to show that a choice that meets these conditions satisfies the ideal of freedom as non-domination. The formula can be interpreted in a way that takes the choice to be a particular choice between certain options—say, going to the theater now rather than staying at home—or as a type of choice—say, the choice that may recur from time to time between going to the theater or staying at home. In most of the discussion I shall leave this more or less harmless ambiguity in play, but it is worth noticing that when we turn in the next chapter to consider the range of choices that should be open to someone who counts as a free person, we shall be concerned with a range of choice-types: for example, the type of choice that arises from time to time in whether to speak your mind, in whether to change job or location, or, indeed, in whether to attend the theater.

A COMMENT ON METHOD

Before looking at the different clauses in our freedom formula, however, I should comment on an objection that may be made to any attempt to settle on a canonical formula of the kind just proposed. The language of freedom is elastic, and the objection is that this elasticity jeopardizes any hope of finding a single, correct paraphrase of what it means to say that you enjoy freedom in the choice between certain options or, to anticipate the next chapter, of what it means to claim that you are a free person.

The objection is worth considering, because the way we talk about freedom is certainly flexible, even wayward. If a citizen is bedridden, we say that he or she still has the freedom to vote. But we also say, in apparent contradiction, that if someone does not have the capacity to enact a certain option like voting, then it's not something in which they have a free choice. Again, we say that you may do something freely—say, decide not to go and vote—even if, unbeknownst to you, all other options are closed: in our example, the polls have shut down. And yet we also say that you do not enjoy freedom in a certain choice if there is only one available alternative—if, in effect, you are forced to take that particular path: whether you know it or not, you cannot now vote. Finally, we say that you have a free choice between two alternatives in a certain domain if those in charge there leave the decision up to you: they allow you to vote, if you wish. And yet we also say that you do not enjoy freedom in a choice if your ability to make the decision depends on someone else granting you permission: if you can decide about whether or not to vote only because they grant you that favor.

While we commonly employ the language of freedom on a flexible pattern, however, this does not imply that freedom-related words and idioms are unconstrained. We cannot, like Humpty Dumpty, make them mean what we wish. Describing a choice or action as free is always meant to mark a contrast with some other choice or action. The same act may count as free in relation to one contrast, unfree in relation to another. Thus, as shifting contexts put different contrasts in play, we may find ourselves ascribing freedom in the one case, unfreedom in another. Take our bedridden citizen on election day. By contrast with a healthy compatriot, our citizen is not free to vote. But by contrast with a non-citizen, it remains perfectly sensible to say that, despite being bedridden, our citizen is indeed free to vote. The predication of freedom is a useful way of marking a contrast in each case, yet the contrast it marks differs between the cases. And so we find ourselves saying apparently contradictory things when, as a matter of fact, they are perfectly consistent.

These observations about the idioms of freedom mean that if we are to build a political theory around the idea of freedom—the idea of what incontrovertibly counts as freedom—then we must regiment things a little and rule on exactly how we are using the term and its cognates. In this and the next chapter, I will attempt to set out the basic understanding of freedom with which I shall be working, trying to make sense of the regimentation I introduce. As already noted, I shall concentrate here on freedom as a property of choices and turn in the next chapter to freedom as a property of persons.

But why embrace the particular conception of freedom that I set out in these chapters? There are three reasons to support it. The first is that it fits with the long-established way of thinking about freedom documented in the previous chapter; it has good historical credentials. The second, as I shall show here, is that it answers very well to the various idioms of freedom we employ in ordinary usage; it has good claims to articulate how we generally think about freedom. And the third is that it provides us with a fruitful ideal of freedom that provides a base for constructing plausible theories of justice, democracy, and sovereignty.

This last consideration is the most important, and it connects with what John Rawls (1971) describes as the test of reflective equilibrium. A theory of freedom will satisfy this test if, on the interpretation of freedom that it defends, the project of promoting freedom makes good political sense: it supports independently attractive proposals in justice, democracy, and sovereignty. Perhaps the best argument for construing freedom on the pattern articulated in this and the next chapter is that that construal turns out to support plausible judgments and policies across these three areas. My hope is that the later chapters of the book will testify convincingly to the claim that those judgments and policies are indeed plausible.

With these preliminaries out of the way, we can begin to examine each of the clauses in the formula for freedom of choice that I outlined earlier. As we look at the arguments for each clause, we will begin to see the appeal of the conception of freedom of choice that they articulate.

Clause 1: You have the room and the resources
to enact the option you prefer

To say that you have the room to enact an option, as I am using the phrase here, is to say that no one interferes with your selection. You have the room to go and cast your vote in an election, assuming you prefer to do so, to the extent that no one makes your selection of that option more or less inaccessible. The government does not interfere with your choice—say, by imposing tests of literacy you do not pass or requiring a form of identification you do not possess. And neither do I or any other agent interfere with the choice—say, by making it difficult for you to get away from work or to find your way to the polls.

If we adopt a standard, generous conception of interference, I may interfere in your choice of a preferred option in any number of ways, all of them presumptively intentional. I may remove the option, blocking your ability to make the choice. I may replace the option by penalizing or burdening it. Or I may misrepresent the option, whether by deceiving you about the available alternatives or manipulating your perception of those alternatives. Thus I may lock you in your room so that you cannot vote; or I may threaten to impose some cost, monetary or otherwise, if you do vote; or I may convince you that today is not election day.[22] The first clause in our account of freedom requires the absence of any such form of interference.

It is important to notice that there are ways in which I may influence your choice without interfering in this sense. I might offer you a reward or trade for not voting, as when, holding a rival party affiliation, I promise that if you do not vote I will not vote either. Or I might present you with some persuasive reason why you should not vote. Incentivizing or persuading you in such a manner does not amount to interference, as I use the term, for it does not remove, replace, or misrepresent the option of not voting or indeed the option of voting. Assuming that you can refuse the trade I offer—it does not mesmerize you like the offer of a drug to an addict—you still face the original options and still retain your capacity to choose. You can choose to vote or not to vote, as you could before, though you now also have a third option of not voting and claiming as a reward that I not vote either. Again, assuming that my effort at persuasion does not involve deception or manipulation, you retain your capacity in that case alone to choose as you wish.

Not only do I avoid interfering in a choice when without deception I seek to persuade you to pick a particular option or offer you a regular trade for doing so; I also avoid interference when without deception I seek to nudge you into choosing a particular option, as it is now sometimes put (Thaler and Sunstein 2008; Sunstein 2013). I might nudge you into voting, as indeed the government might do so, by presenting voting as an act of civic virtue, by arranging things on the presupposition that you will want to vote, or just by making it easy to go and vote. Nudging will preserve your freedom in making the choice insofar as it does not remove or replace any option and, not being deceptive, does not impair your capacity to choose between the options.

Few are likely to contest the linkage between free choice and the enjoyment of the room or noninterference that choice requires. But the first clause of the formula also introduces a second, more demanding linkage, requiring that in addition to the room to enact your preferred option, you should also have the resources necessary to enact it (Van Parijs 1995). Some opponents of this requirement object that you can be said to be free to take an option—say, because you are legally entitled to take it—even when you do not have the required resources. Thus, to revert to an earlier example, they might say that as a citizen you are free to vote even if you suffer a crippling incapacity that keeps you from the polls (Berlin 1969, 122). But it would be a mistake to think that such examples support a general disconnection between being free to do something and having the resources needed to do it. The usage illustrated in the voting case, as we saw earlier, is explained by the contextual, contrastive purpose it serves.

As it happens, there is a quite general reason for keeping the connection between freedom and resources. Assume that if you are free to choose an option, then you can be held responsible for making or not making the choice: you can be blamed or praised, depending on the merits of the alternative (Pettit 2001c). This means that whether you are free to choose an option turns in part on whether you are fit to be held responsible for making or not making the choice: such fitness is a necessary condition for freedom. But if you recognize that you do not have the resources to choose a certain option—if you realize that you are too sick to go to the polls—then you must admit that you are not fit to be held responsible for failing to take it; you have a perfectly good excuse for the failure. And so, if you recognize that you lack the required resources, you must equally admit that you were not free to choose the option in question: you were not in that sense free to vote. The belief that you have the freedom to choose a certain option requires you to believe that you have all the resources needed for choosing it.

What exactly are the resources necessary to enact a given option? They fall into three broad areas: personal, natural, and social. In each of these areas you must have certain objective resources at your disposal. And in each area those resources must be at your conscious disposal—they must register with you cognitively—for otherwise you would not be positioned to make use of them.

The personal resources required for enacting any option cover the mental and bodily ability or knowhow needed to make the choice, and the awareness of having such a capacity. You must be consciously able to go to the polls or, to return to earlier examples, consciously able to raise your hand, or consciously know how to send an email. In Thomas Hobbes's (1994b, 21.2) phrase, you must have the "strength and wit" to enact the option.

The natural resources required to enact a preferred option are those conditions in your environment that would put the option within reach. In order to raise your hand, it must not be so cold that you are paralyzed or believe yourself to be paralyzed. In order to send an email, there must not be an electrical storm that knocks out the Internet or leads you to think that the Internet is knocked out. And in order to vote, there must be an election booth within reach of where you live and you must know that this is the case.

What now of social resources? When you raise your hand, considered just as a physical movement, there are no particular social resources needed. But such resources will be necessary for using your raised hand to signal something. You will be able to raise your hand to greet someone, or to call a foul in umpiring a game, only if your society establishes conventions that, as a matter of shared awareness, make such an act of communication possible. Even more obviously, of course, you will be able to send an email—or make a telephone call or mail a letter—only if your society manifestly provides you with the requisite technology and infrastructure: routers, switches, a postal service, and so on. Similarly, you will be able to vote only if your country's law puts a suitable electoral system in place.

How far such social resources extend may be unclear. Consider a case where you are able to raise your hand only with the help of a physiotherapist who is coaching you back to health after an accident, or where you are able to send an email only with the assistance of a tech-savvy colleague. Do you have the ability in such a case to take the option mentioned? Does the voluntary assistance of another person count as a relevant social resource?

My response is that if you depend on the goodwill of a given individual or set of individuals for being able to take the relevant option, then you do not have the ability to take the option in the sense required for freedom. You will have the ability required for free choice only if others are independently constrained to provide the assistance you need, or if there is a queue of people willing to provide it so that, should any assistants fail, there will be others willing to take their place. But you will not have that ability just because someone happens to be willing to help you at a given moment in time. This formulation is plausible insofar as there is a clear distinction between the case where you depend on the goodwill of others for assistance and the case in which you can command such assistance, as we might say—the case where you can lay claim to it, as if it were yours to own. That distinction will be relevant later when we consider the conditions under which domination occurs; the first case allows domination, as we shall see, while the second does not.

Clause 2: Whatever your own preference over those options

According to the first clause in our account, you enjoy freedom in choosing between certain options only to the extent that you have the room and the resources to enact the option you prefer. According to the second clause, you enjoy freedom in your choice only if every option is accessible in that way, and not just the option you happen to prefer. Think of the options in the choice, in a metaphor given currency by Isaiah Berlin (1969), as each representing a door through which you might pass. What the second clause requires is that every door should be open, not just the door you happen to push on.

In 1651, Thomas Hobbes (1994b, 21.2) argued in favor of a version of the first clause in our account of freedom. He maintained that someone is free to choose a certain option only if the person is "not hindered"—in our terms, not interfered with—in making that choice and, in addition, only if the option involved figures amongst "those things which by his strength and wit he is able to do." But even though he construes the requirements of freedom in line with the first clause in our formula for freedom, he offers a good example of someone who construes them in a manner that is inconsistent with the second.

Hobbes takes this position in requiring not just that the free agent is not hindered, but more specifically that he "is not hindered to do what he has a will to": that is, is not hindered to do what he prefers to do. In stating the requirement in that manner, Hobbes implies that an agent can enjoy freedom in a choice, despite being hindered or obstructed from taking options other than the one he actually prefers. While he requires that the door you push on should be open, allowing you to pass through, he does not require that all the other doors should be open too.

For all that his notion of freedom requires, those doors may be locked or jammed or made difficult to access in other ways.[23]

Since we often associate freedom with getting your own way and escaping the frustration of your preference, Hobbes's view has a certain appeal. But as a general account of what freedom demands, it is exposed to a powerful objection. The objection is well put by Berlin, who argues that the Hobbesian view leads to an absurdity.[24] If someone imposes restrictions on you that frustrate your preference, you can make yourself free just by adapting your preferences appropriately; you do not have to go to the trouble of lifting the imposed restrictions.

Suppose that you are in prison, for example, and desperately want to live in the outside world, so that by the Hobbesian account you are frustrated and unfree. Conscious of your frustration, you begin to work on your own psychology. You focus on all the good things about prison life: the regular hours, the reliable shelter, the chance to read and think and perhaps to improve yourself. In time you come to like being in prison, preferring a stretch behind bars to living in the uncertain world outside. Well then, by the Hobbesian account, you will thereby have made yourself free. Between the option of staying in prison and the option of living outside, you get what you now have come to prefer.

It is absurd to think that merely by adapting your preferences, you could liberate yourself in a choice such as the one between life behind bars and life on the street. Liberation in that sort of situation requires an alteration in the situation under which you live; it cannot come about merely by an alteration in attitude. To think that it could come about in that way would be to confuse removing frustration with achieving freedom. As Berlin (1969, xxxix) says, "To teach a man that, if he cannot get what he wants, he must learn to want only what he can get may contribute to his happiness or his security; but it will not increase his civil or political freedom."

The lesson is that we should endorse the second as well as the first clause in our account of freedom. There may be contexts in which people who get what they want could be described as enjoying freedom. But it would be quite misleading to think that in general this is enough for freedom. To have a free choice between certain options, you must be positioned to get whichever option you might want, however unlikely it is that you might want it. All of the doors in the choice must be open to you. It will not be enough to want the one option that, as it happens, you are positioned to get—to push on the one door that just happens to lie ajar.

Clause 3: Whatever the preference of any other
as to how you should choose

Under the first clause of our formula, you are not free to choose between certain options unless you have the room and the resources to enact the option you prefer. Under the second, you are not free to choose between the options unless you have the room and the resources to enact any of the options you might prefer, not just the option you actually happen to prefer. Under the third clause, you are not free to choose between the options unless you are positioned to choose in a more robust measure still. Your capacity to enact the option you prefer must remain in place not only if you change your mind about what to choose, but also if others change their minds as to what you should choose.[25]

Where Hobbes illustrates the position of someone who endorses the first claim but rejects the second, Isaiah Berlin illustrates the position of someone who endorses the second claim but not the third.[26] For all that he says about the importance of each option in your choice remaining an open door, in his formulation it does not matter that the options might be open only because of my goodwill or favor, where I am a powerful presence in your life. It does not matter that I am in the position of a doorkeeper—say, a burly bouncer—who can slam any door in your face; it does not matter that I have such dominating power over you.

According to the third clause, the freedom of a choice requires not only that all the options in the choice should be open doors, as Berlin holds, but also that there should be no doorkeeper. Torvald, to return to the example from Ibsen, is a doorkeeper in respect of Nora's choices. He may let her choose between going to the theater with a friend and staying at home with him, but he has the power to close either door should he wish, asserting his rights under nineteenth-century law and custom. Nora depends on his goodwill for each of the doors to remain ajar. If there is a doorkeeper that monitors your choices, as Torvald monitors Nora's, then in making those choices you will not act solely on your own will. You may be able to satisfy whatever your will happens to be, but you will have this capacity only because the doorkeeper makes it so. You will be subject to that person's reserve control and all you will enjoy is free rein, not freedom in the fullest sense.

Will it make a difference if Torvald not only allows Nora latitude in a given situation, but is extremely unlikely ever to want to limit it; if he gives her free rein and will almost certainly continue to do so? That he may never turn nasty increases Nora's prospect of getting what she wants but, according to the third clause, it will not give her any greater freedom. For while it may be improbable that Torvald should change his attitude or behavior toward Nora, it remains within his power as a free agent to do so. Thus, no matter how likely Torvald is to continue to dote on his wife, she remains dependent on him as on a doorkeeper who can shut down any of her options.

How do we defend this third clause in our account of freedom of choice, vindicating the republican way of thinking? The most straightforward defense draws on an assumption that retains an intuitive appeal, even two centuries after the eclipse of republicanism. This is the assumption that you cannot be free in making a choice if you make it in subjection to the will of another agent, whether or not you are conscious of the subjection. You will certainly be subject to my will when I impose on you by interfering with some of your options. But the republican insight is that you will also be subject to my will in the case where I let you choose the option you prefer—and would have let you choose any option you preferred—but only because I happen to want you to enjoy such latitude. If your capacity to choose one or other of the options is not robust over changes in my will or preference as to how you should choose—if it remains present only so long as I continue to indulge you with my goodwill—then I am in ultimate control, not you. However indulgent I may be, it remains that you will be able to choose according to your own will only insofar as I give you leave to do so; you will be able to make your choice only *cum permissu*, as it used to be said, only with my permission.[27]

We can buttress the case for including the third clause in our account of freedom with an argument that parallels Berlin's reasoning about the second claim (Pettit 2011). As we saw, Berlin argues that if freedom is available just in the absence of frustration, then you can make yourself free in a given choice by adapting your preferences; you can liberate yourself from a life behind bars by coming to prefer it to life on the streets. This shows that if Hobbes is right—if the mere absence of frustration is enough for freedom of choice—then, absurdly, liberation by adaptation is possible. But if Berlin is right—if the absence of interference with any option is enough for freedom of choice—then a similar absurdity follows: liberation by ingratiation is equally possible. You can free yourself by taking steps that traditionally signal subjection and unfreedom, resorting to the arts of fawning and flattery in the hope of mollifying those with the power to interfere in your affairs.

Consider the choice between voting and not voting. Suppose I can and do put an obstacle in the way of your voting: I am your employer and insist that if you go to vote—perhaps taking time off work—I will fire you. If just the absence of interference on my part will give you freedom in that choice, then you may be able to achieve such freedom by kowtowing or toadying or cozying up to me, winning my grace and favor through sycophancy and self-abasement. You will bring about this result insofar as I am warmed and charmed by your attentions, and am happy to reward you by abstaining from interference in the choice and letting you act on your preference. But it is absurd to think that you can make yourself free by indulging in a form of ingratiation that is the very hallmark of subjection. Your ingratiation may win you permission to vote or not to vote, as you please, but it does not release you from subjection to my will; on the contrary, it comes about via an overt acknowledgment of your dependency on my wishes.

This point is particularly salient when we ask whether you are free to vote or not to vote, as a general type of choice—a type that recurs routinely in local, provincial, and national elections—rather than asking whether you were free to vote or not to vote on a particular occasion. If you managed in this or that election to win your way with me, your employer, and persuaded me to let you do what you wish, then we might be willing to think that you achieved freedom in that particular instance. But suppose that when it comes to voting as a type of activity or choice, you have the freedom to vote or not to vote only insofar as I allow you to do so. In that case it would be downright misleading to suggest that just because I am generally indulgent—perhaps as a result of your powers of ingratiation—you do enjoy such freedom. The point is well put by Berlin when, veering momentarily toward a conception of freedom as non-domination, he says that the person who is free in certain types of choices "is not obliged to account for his activities to any man" (Berlin 1969, lx). Clearly you would be obliged to account for your activities to me if you depended on my permission to be able to vote. You would not enjoy the freedom associated with citizenship.

The point can also be illustrated by a variant on the case of Nora and Torvald. Suppose that Torvald is actually a nasty type and tends to want to frustrate Nora's presumptive preference in one or another type of choice. And now imagine that Nora wins her way in a given area by resort to the mincing steps and beguiling smiles that the eighteenth-century feminist Mary Wollstonecraft (1982) associated with female subordination. Does Nora enjoy freedom in the exercise of a given type of choice—say, to revert to our earlier example, as she manages to coax Torvald into allowing her to attend the theater regularly with a friend? Surely not. This is not freedom at its incontrovertible best, only what Edmund Burke (1970, 77), echoing republican ideas, described in a speech of 1773 as "liberty under a connivance." It does not remove Nora's subjection to Torvald's will or preference. On the contrary, it comes about by means of an open acceptance of her dependency on that will: an admission that if she can take a certain sort of option, or if she can choose between certain sorts of options, that is only because Torvald happens to allow it.

If the freedom to choose between options is not required to survive changes in the preferences of others as to what you should do, then it will make sense to think that freedom can be won by means of ingratiation. But this is an absurd thing to claim, as our examples suggest; it mirrors the absurdity in the parallel claim that freedom might be won by preference adaptation. And so we have to reject the thesis that makes the absurdity inescapable. We have to agree that freedom involves the ability to enact any of the options in a choice, regardless not only of what you prefer to choose, but also of what others prefer that you choose.

FREEDOM AS NON-DOMINATION

The conception of freedom in a choice that emerges from the three clauses in our formula is a regimented version of the republican ideal of freedom as non-domination. The first two clauses identify common assumptions made by republican writers: that free choice presupposes the resources as well as the room for choosing what you prefer; and that it presupposes such a resourced capacity for choice, not just with the option you happen to prefer, but with any of the options in the choice. The third clause in the formula goes on to pick up the most distinctive and important element on which republicans focused.

This third clause, of course, states that any dependence on the goodwill of another for being able to choose as you wish is inimical to freedom. You do not enjoy freedom of choice, according to this way of thinking, when your ability to choose is dependent on the state of another's will as to how you should choose, be that other an individual agent like me or an agency such as a church or company or state. You will be unfree in such a choice, as the eighteenth-century republican Richard Price (1991, 26) put it, because your access to the options will depend on an "indulgence" or an "accidental mildness" in the more powerful agent or agency. Freedom in the republican sense, to quote the seventeenth-century thinker Algernon Sidney (1990, 17, 304), requires something much more robust: "independency upon the will of another," or, as he also puts it, "exemption from dominion" by another. The upshot is well caught in *Cato's Letters,* the radical eighteenth-century tract: "Liberty is, to live upon one's own terms; slavery is, to live at the mere mercy of another" (Trenchard and Gordon 1971, vol. 2, 249–50).

Republican writers such as Price and Sidney took it for granted that the first two clauses in our formula for freedom are necessary, and laid particular stress on the third. But, while those two clauses are independently defensible, as we have seen, we should notice that in any case it would be hard to uphold the third clause—the need for non-domination—and not maintain them as well. In any significant choice where you do not satisfy the first two clauses, you are likely to fail the third clause as well, falling under the domination of another.

Take any choice that is important for you to be able to make, whether in speaking out about something, making common cause with others, or taking up a job offer. Non-domination in such a choice certainly requires escaping interference with whatever option you happen to prefer, thereby enjoying the room needed to make the choice; if you do not escape interference then you are under the power of the interferer. But arguably it also requires having the resources necessary to enact whatever option you might prefer. If you lacked those resources, yet needed to make the choice, then you would have to depend on the good graces of another to provide you with those resources. And that would be to put the other in a position to dominate you: they would be able to withdraw their assistance at any point and so would enjoy a power of interference in your exercise of the choice.

But the third clause does not merely support the first two clauses in our formula. It also has crucial implications for the interpretation of those claims. The two clauses present the absence of interference by others—that is, the room for choice—and the presence of required resources as equally important factors in the freedom of choice. The third clause introduces an asymmetry between those factors. It says that interference must be robustly absent: that is, absent over variations in how far others are hostile or friendly. But it does not require that resources—that is, the personal, natural, and social resources that happen to be at your disposal—must be present over variations in your personal skills, the natural environment, or the structure of society. In order to choose freely between the options in a certain choice, it is enough that you actually have such assets available; there is no requirement that they should continue to be available, for example, under various disaster scenarios.

This difference in attitude toward the absence of interference on the one hand and the presence of resources on the other reflects the thesis, central to the republican way of thinking, that it is inherently worse to be controlled by the free will of another than to be constrained by a contingent absence of resources.[28] That thesis is given great prominence by Immanuel Kant, someone broadly aligned with the tradition but influenced in particular by Jean-Jacques Rousseau. Kant (2005, 11) remarks in notes written after reading Rousseau's *Social Contract*:

"Find himself in what condition he will, the human being is dependent on many external things . . . But what is harder and more unnatural than this yoke of necessity is the subjection of one human being under the will of another. No misfortune can be more terrifying to one who is accustomed to freedom."

The independence from the will of another that is required under the republican conception of freedom may seem to argue for driving wedges between individuals, setting each up in a solipsistic sort of independence from society in general or from other people in particular. But this would be completely misleading. Republican freedom is meant to exemplify the freedom of the city, as we saw at the end of the last chapter, not the freedom of the heath.

In underlining this theme, there are three points to make about the requirement that you should be able to choose as you wish regardless of the preferences of others as to how you should choose. First, you are not required to be able to choose as you wish regardless of the preferences of others on independent or orthogonal matters, only regardless of their preferences on the issue of what you or your kind should choose. Second, you are not required to be able to choose as you wish regardless of what count by accepted standards as the constrained or involuntary preferences of others, only regardless of preferences in which others have a degree of discretion and can be moved by their attitude toward you. And third, you are not required to be able to choose as you wish regardless of the preferences of others whom you yourself voluntarily invest with the power and right of shaping your choices. These points deserve a little attention because, while they may come across as excessively theoretical, they have important policy implications, as we shall see later.

Suppose, to take up the first point, that you'd like to fly overseas for the weekend. Your ability to get to your destination depends on the preferences of others in the sense that there would not be an airline network if others were averse to flight. Does this mean that the third clause is breached and that even if you get away as planned, you do so unfreely? Certainly not. You do not depend on the preferences of any other as to what you should choose but only on an orthogonal pattern of preference that is as indifferent to what you choose as the patterns in the weather. The third clause associates freedom with independence from the will of others only in the sense in which this means not being dependent on their goodwill toward you or yours, and that is consistent with being dependent for the opportunities you face on the general preferences of others in your society. Freedom requires not having to depend on the indulgence or permission of others to act as you wish. It does not require independence of their preferences in other matters or of the social resources, such as an airplane network, that reflect those preferences.

Turning to the second of our three points, suppose your weekend getaway depends on a bank's judgment about whether you can afford to take the overseas trip and on the preference it might form on that basis for lending you the necessary funds. Imagine the bank agrees that you can have those funds, on the grounds that your credit history makes this feasible. Does the fact that the bank might have made a different judgment, and might therefore have obstructed your plan, mean that even in the case where you do go, you do not adopt that option in full freedom; you operate under the will of a dominating agency? Surely not. In this scenario, the bank is merely doing what banks have to do—or so we may assume—by local standards that bear on their role: it is determining how to treat you, on the basis of accepted criteria for good loans. Any preference the bank or the bank's officials might have as to how you in particular should fare is preempted by the constraint of that policy. Whether the bank offers you funds or denies you funds, it does not act on the basis of a voluntary preference as to how you should act. Being constrained to act on the basis of accepted standards of banking, it operates like a force of nature, not like an agent whose attitudes toward you can determine how you fare.[29]

The final point to make about the independence from the will of others that is associated with freedom as non-domination is more simple and straightforward than the previous two. In order to illustrate this point, imagine that you are in the habit of making impulsive trips overseas and that in an attempt to curb your impulses you have entrusted me with your passport. Imagine, in particular, that you have done this with the instruction that on no account should I return the passport to you for an immediate trip, only for a trip that is at least a week away. It is certainly true in this case that you will be dependent on my will for whether or not you can take the trip you are currently excited about. But does that mean that you are dominated and unfree? Surely not. Considered as an agent of the moment, you are subject to my will, but considered as an agent who endures through time, it is your will and not mine that authorizes my action and exercises ultimate control. You voluntarily maintain your subjection to me, since you can suspend it at a week's notice. Besides, you can change the arrangement if you wish: you can reduce the requirement of a week's notice, for example, to twenty-four hours' notice.

These three points all reflect the fact that the dependence that is inconsistent with freedom in a choice, as registered in the final clause of our formula, is restricted to a distinctively inimical kind of dependence. This is the dependence that puts you in the power of others, enabling them to decide on whether or not to interfere in your choices, on the basis of their attitude toward you or your kind, and without having your permission or license to treat you in that way. Such dependence on others contrasts with the innocent forms of dependence that expose you to the orthogonal or constrained or authorized preferences of others. These forms of dependence are part and parcel of social life and are fully consistent with freedom as non-domination. The ideal of freedom as non-domination presupposes life in the company of others, with all the restrictions associated with the orthogonal, constrained, and authorized preferences of others. What it rules out is exposure in the course of social life to the inimical dependence that puts you under the will of others in the way in which Nora is put under the will of Torvald.

DEGREES AND KINDS OF DOMINATION

The fact that domination is enough to deprive you of freedom in a choice, as entailed by the third clause, does not mean that domination is all of a kind, equally objectionable in every variety. Domination with interference—the sort that Torvald would practice if he turned nasty—is clearly worse than domination without interference: that is, the domination that the doting, indulgent Torvald imposes.[30] It imposes tighter restrictions on choice. Thus the claim that freedom in a choice requires non-domination is quite consistent with an admission that when your freedom fails, it may fail in a more or less serious measure.

Freedom may not only fail in a more or less serious measure for this reason. It may also fail because the interference that domination makes possible is more or less seriously constraining. We saw that I may interfere in your choice by removing one or another option, by replacing one or another option by a penalized counterpart or by misrepresenting the options available, deceiving you about them or manipulating your perception of them. Such forms of interference vary in how far they make a choice impossible or difficult or costly. And as they vary in these ways, so does the extent to which my power or exercise of interference imposes limits on your will and reduces your freedom.

But not only may domination be worse for being attended by interference. And not only may it be worse for being attended by a more rather than a less intrusive form of interference. It may also be worse for being supported by a less easily remediable rather than a more easily remediable form of power. The power of a husband like Torvald is going to be less easily remediable in a society that does not allow divorce than in a society that does.

These observations have implications for how we should direct resources in the protection of people's freedom, and will be relevant in the consideration of issues of policy in the second part of the book. But there is one further remark we should add, since it bears also on policy matters.

The republican focus does not necessarily mean that in seeking to protect people against domination we should attend primarily to the particular relationships in which they suffer domination, whether at the hands of other individuals or of corporate agencies such as companies, churches, and states. Such domination is often possible only because of the practices and institutions of the wider society and world: the culture, economy, or constitution under which people live. It will often make sense in pursuing relief from domination to pay attention to these deeper sources of subjection. They make for what we might describe as structural domination, as distinct from the relational domination to which we give prominence in defining freedom (Hayward 2011). The republican requirements of social justice, which we will explore shortly, are directed in good part at negating the relational effects of such structural domination.

The propositions defended in this chapter bring us close to being able to address more concrete policy issues of justice, democracy, and sovereignty. But we need to spend a little more time on abstract, philosophical matters, for we still have to connect our discussion of what it means for a particular choice, or a particular sort of choice, to be free with what it means for a person to be free. The ideal of the free, undominated person, not just the ideal of free choice, must guide us on what is required for justice, democracy, and sovereignty. I address this fuller ideal in chapter 3, asking about the range of choices in which we should expect people to be resourced and protected if they are to count as free persons. Where chapter 2 has provided us with a sense of the depth of resourcing and protection required for freedom in a particular choice, chapter 3 will provide us with an appreciation of the breadth of choice across which it ought to be provided.

Chapter 3

FREEDOM WITH BREADTH

We concentrated in the last chapter on what it might mean, at its best, to enjoy freedom in a particular choice or type of choice. But the freedom you enjoy in this or that choice does not necessarily make for a great benefit. And certainly it need not make for such a great benefit that you count intuitively as a free person. Imagine a society that gave each person freedom in only a single type of choice. One society might allow you to wear whatever clothes appeal to you; another might allow you and others to take one or another preferred route to work; yet another might allow you to decide between certain jobs in the local place of employment. Such fantastical regimes would do no better for their inhabitants than the repressive, dystopian world imagined in George Orwell's novel *1984*. Their inhabitants would be slaves of the community, not in any sense free persons.

This example, however extreme or improbable, teaches a simple lesson. In order to count as a free person, you need more than free choice in this or that type of decision. Indeed, you need more than free choice in any randomly chosen decisions, however numerous. Being able to choose freely in all of the three choices mentioned, for example—being free to choose

what to wear, how to travel to work, and which job to take—
would not make you a free person either. How, then, should we
determine the range of choices in which you must enjoy freedom in order to count, intuitively, as a free person? We know
that the freedom you enjoy must have the depth described in
the last chapter; it must involve the resources and protections
associated with freedom as non-domination. We now have to
settle on the breadth of choice—the range of decisions in which
such freedom should be available.[31]

THE FREE CITIZEN

The tradition of republican thought provides indispensable
assistance in this quest. Central to that tradition, as already
mentioned, is the image of the *liber* or freeman: the person who
lives *sui juris,* on his own terms. A free citizen, in this sense,
enjoyed a legal or civic status in relation to others—others in both
their private and public capacity—that gave that person independence from their will in exercising certain personal choices. This
status was available in previous ages only to an elite citizenry,
of course—a citizenry of mainstream, propertied males—but it
offers us a model of what an inclusive citizenry ought to be able
to enjoy. It gives us a plausible sense of the broad front on which
freedom as non-domination ought to be assured.

The status needed for being a free person under the received
republican conception imposes objective and subjective requirements. It requires that you should be objectively secure against
the intrusions of others, including the intrusions of the very
government that protects you against others. In particular, it
requires security in what John Lilburne (1646), a radical republican of the seventeenth century, described as the fundamental

liberties. Later we will consider carefully the types of choices that ought to be encompassed in the fundamental liberties, but by all accounts they include freedom of speech, religion, association, and the like. Being secure against intrusion in such choices means, in the ideal, that you are objectively safeguarded and supported against any agent or agency that might take against you, regardless of how likely they are to do so. You have all the room and the resources that are required for the exercise of such choices, independently of the attitudes of the powerful toward you.

But the status of the free person, as encoded in the traditional image of the *liber* or freeman, has a subjective as well as an objective side. It requires that you be securely resourced and protected against others, yes, but it also requires that this entrenchment register as a matter of common awareness. Everyone must be aware that you are secured in this way, everyone must be aware that this is a matter of general awareness, and so on; your status must be salient and manifest to all. Only then can you walk tall among your fellows, conscious of sharing in the general recognition that no one can push you around—as no one can push anyone around—and expect to escape censure or penalty.

This idea of a subjective register inherent in republicanism played an important role in the traditional model of the free citizen. As Thomas Hobbes (1994b, 10.5) noted in another context, the "reputation of power is power." Potential offenders recognize that you have objectively secured rights. And the recognition of those rights—in particular, the recognition in common with others of those rights—reinforces the very protection you enjoy; it is likely to inhibit any temptation that others might feel to offend against you.

John Lilburne gave vivid expression to this idea that freedom involves an objective but subjectively registered status. A supporter of the new English republic, he wrote in the 1640s that "the freeman's freedom" means that all citizens should be equal in legal power and equal in the recognition and dignity that this would confer; they ought to be "equal and alike in power, dignity, authority, and majesty—none of them having (by nature) any authority, dominion or magisterial power, one over or above another" (Sharp 1998). The somewhat less radical John Milton (1953–82, vol. 8, 424–25) endorsed broadly the same idea when he argued in that same period that in a "free Commonwealth," "they who are greatest . . . are not elevated above their brethren; live soberly in their families, walk the streets as other men, may be spoken to freely, familiarly, friendly, without adoration."

The republican tradition has always insisted that the objective and subjective status invoked by Lilburne and Milton is only available under a public rule of law in which all are treated as equals, being offered the same resources of choice and the same protections against the intrusion of others. The laws required cover many areas that are distinguished in contemporary jurisprudence, though not always in traditional. Thus, as we shall see later in this chapter, the law of property and contract is needed to establish our understanding of the basic liberties, as indeed is the law of torts: this determines the limits beyond which people are not entitled to impose risks on others. Criminal law, family law, and employment law are required to play a vital role in protecting various liberties, as we shall see in the next chapter. And constitutional law is important in giving people shared and individual control over the system for introducing such laws, as we shall see in chapter 7.

But the republican tradition did not rely solely on laws to provide the security required for freedom. Social norms have always been assumed to play a vital, supportive role in making laws effective. Thus Machiavelli (1965) remarks in *Discourses* 1.18 on the importance of the support that norms or morals provide for laws, and indeed on the importance of the reciprocal support that laws provide for norms: "just as good morals, if they are to be maintained, have need of the laws, so the laws, if they are to be observed, have need of good morals."

The social norms that support laws, doubling the objective and subjective security that the laws underwrite, consist by most accounts in patterns of behavior that people expect to be approved of for displaying and disapproved of for not displaying.[32] These are patterns, moreover, that that expectation helps to keep in place, leading people generally to conform to them (Brennan and Pettit 2004; Pettit 2008b; Appiah 2010). Thus social norms are distinct from mere standards, which are more honored in the breach than the observance, such as the standard of bipartisanship in politics. But equally they are distinct from mere regularities that are not expected to attract either approval or disapproval, such as the regularity of sleeping at night rather than during the day. Like mere regularities, norms are patterns to which people do generally conform; and like mere standards, they are patterns that are expected to trigger suitable forms of approval and disapproval. What distinguishes them is that they are patterns that attract conformity and that do so, at least partly, because of the expectation—manifest to all—that conformity triggers approval, nonconformity disapproval.[33]

There is no surprise in the idea that social norms might reinforce laws, or at least laws that treat each as equal and promote a good for all. Since any offenses can undermine the contribution of these laws, potential transgressors can expect that others, being themselves supported and protected by the laws, will disapprove not only of an offense against themselves, but also of any offense against a third party. And the desire to avoid general disapproval—and the corresponding desire to win approval—is bound to offer potential offenders a motive to comply with the laws over and beyond the motive of avoiding legal punishment. The prospect of shame at being found to have cheated in your tax return, or to have misled or hurt others in some way, will be as powerful a deterrent as the prospect of any penalty that the legal system may impose. Thus the community will police potential offenders into compliance with the law by exposing each to the prospect of disapproval—and to the costs associated with disapproval—in the event they do not comply.[34]

Social norms may support the law not only by providing incentives to conform to particular appealing laws, but also in two other ways. They may support certain patterns of behavior, such as telling the truth or keeping promises, in a variety of different contexts, not just in the special cases—for example, in the courtroom or in formal contracts—where coercive law is useful. And they may support conformity to the law—say, because of its beneficial coordinating effects—even in cases where many members of the population believe that the laws in place are less than ideal (Raz 1986).

To sum up, then, the republican ideal of the free citizen holds that in order to be a free citizen you must enjoy non-domination in such a range of choice, and on the basis of such public resourcing and protection, that you stand on a par with others. You must enjoy a freedom secured by public laws and norms in the range of the fundamental or basic liberties. And in that sense, you must count as equal with the best.

Free citizens in this image do not have to depend on anyone's grace or favor for being able to choose their mode of life. And they relate to one another in a shared, mutually reinforcing consciousness of enjoying this independence; they share in the good of reciprocal recognition (Honneth 1996; McBride 2013). Thus, in the established terms of republican denigration, they do not have to bow or scrape, toady or kowtow, fawn or flatter; they do not have to placate others with beguiling smiles or mincing steps. They do not have to live on their wits or walk on eggshells. They are their own men and women and however deeply they bind themselves to one another, as in love or friendship or trust, they do so as a matter of voluntary choice, reaching out to one another from positions of relatively equal strength.

WHAT ARE THE BASIC LIBERTIES?

What are the basic liberties that should be associated with a free civic status? What are the types of choice that ought to be resourced and protected on the basis of public laws and norms if the members of a contemporary society are to enjoy the status or dignity of the free republican citizen?

The idea of the basic liberties figures prominently in contemporary political theory. The dominant approach to identifying them, which I have followed up to this point, consists in offering a few examples—say, the liberties of speech, religion, and association—and using these to exemplify the whole class. But that approach to the basic liberties is unhelpfully vague, as is the rival approach that would cast them as the liberties required for being able to realize your moral personality, exercising the capacity for rational choice and reasonable accommodation with others (Rawls 1993). I prefer a third alternative, which relies on the republican image of the free person—the *liber* or freeman—to help us identify the choice-types that ought to be resourced and protected as basic liberties. This image identifies the relevant choices by their satisfaction of a floor constraint on the one side, a ceiling constraint on the other.

The ceiling constraint is that the basic liberties should not include choices that put people at loggerheads with one another and force them into competition. If the members of a society are each to have the status of a free person, then the choices in which they are safeguarded ought to be restricted to choices that they can each enjoy at the same time that others enjoy them. If people had to compete with others to gain access to the basic liberties—if they had to compete in the way in which people compete for prizes—then there would be winners and losers. Not all of the participants could enjoy the range of choice associated with being a free person.

The floor constraint is that the basic liberties should encompass all the choices that are co-enjoyable in this sense, not just a subset of them.[35] Imagine that a society provides for some members of a set of choices available in principle to everyone, but not for all. Suppose it leaves out freedom of expression or movement, for example, where there is no deep problem about establishing that extra liberty in addition to the others. The citizens of such a society could hardly count as free persons in the fullest sense; they would be unnecessarily hampered in the range of activities accessible to them.

What choices are likely to be co-enjoyable by all in a given society and fit, therefore, to be publicly entrenched there as basic liberties: fit to be supported by publicly delivered resources and protections? If a set of choices is to be co-enjoyable by all, I suggest, then it must meet two conditions. First, people must be able to exercise any one of the choices in the set, no matter how many others are exercising it at the same time; each choice must be co-exercisable. And second, people must be able, so far as possible, to derive satisfaction from the exercise of any choice, no matter how many others are exercising that choice, or any other choice in the set, at the same time; the set of choices as a whole must be co-satisfying.

The task before us, then, is to identify in a general way the co-exercisable, co-satisfying choices that ought to be secured or entrenched as basic liberties under a republican dispensation. In approaching this task, we can take advantage of the fact that some candidates are upstream from others and that we need only focus on choices in the upstream domain. One choice will be upstream from a second if the fact that we entrench the first means that we entrench the second, but not vice versa. If we entrench your freedom to tell me what you think, then we entrench your freedom to tell me about your holiday plans, but not vice versa; you might be free to tell me about your holiday plans, after all, without being free to tell me what you think more generally. If we entrench your freedom to tell any audience what you think, then we entrench your freedom to let me in particular know what you think, but not vice versa; you might be free to tell me what you think without being free to tell any others. The choice in the first position within each pair is upstream from the choice in the second. In considering the co-exercisable, co-satisfying choices that ought to be entrenched under a republican arrangement, we need only consider the upstream candidates: specifically, the co-enjoyable choices that are not downstream from any other co-enjoyable choices. If the laws and norms secure or entrench freedom in the upstream choices in any area, then by necessity they will entrench all downstream choices as well.

WHAT CHOICES ARE CO-EXERCISABLE?

Many choices are incapable of being exercised by people at the same time, because some or all people are incapable of exercising them, period. No one can be sure of being able to choose to do something that requires special skills, for example, as in climbing high mountains or mastering string theory. And no one can be sure of being able to choose to do something that involves the cooperation of another; without a willing partner, you cannot tango. Thus, the only choices that ought to be entrenched as basic liberties are choices that are within everyone's reach acting just on their own, or that are within everyone's reach with some basic assistance from common resources.[36] People can be assured of the freedom to enact options within their personal control in that sense, but they cannot be assured of the freedom to enact an option that requires special skills or the cooperation of others.

This restriction is not as severe as it may seem at first. While we cannot entrench your freedom to go mountain climbing, we can entrench your freedom of movement within the society. So if you have the suitable skills, you are free to climb in the local mountains. And while we cannot legally or otherwise entrench your freedom to tango, or your freedom to associate in any way with others, we can entrench a freedom to tango or associate with anyone who will welcome an association with you. In entrenching the freedom of that choice, of course, we will have entrenched your and your dance partner's freedom to tango together, even though this is not a choice that either of you can make on your own.[37]

Any choices to be entrenched as basic liberties, then, should be limited to the things that any normal, able-minded adult can do on their own in any normal, habitable environment, at least with assistance from a common pool of resources. They will include choices like those we exercise when we think for ourselves, communicate our thoughts, associate with willing partners in various ways, make a living for ourselves, and travel about within our society.

Moving beyond this first restriction, however, other choices fail to be co-exercisable because their exercise by some people means that others cannot exercise the same choice at more or less the same time. Logic dictates that not everyone can be chief of his or her village, not everyone can be famous, and not everyone can score above average, even in Lake Wobegon. So we cannot entrench the freedom to achieve fame, for example, as distinct from the freedom to try to be famous.

As logic means that necessarily these choices are not co-exercisable by all, so scarce resources can exert the same effect on a variety of other choices. The farmer and the cowboy might be less at odds if there were country enough for them each to find land that they can use as they wish; the farmer would fence in one region, the cowboy let cattle roam in another. But a finite amount of land means that they cannot each have an entrenched freedom to use the land as they wish.[38] Similarly, pedestrians, cyclists, and motorists might be able to roam free if there were space enough for each of them to find routes that caused no problems for others. But in a world where roads and paths are scarce resources, they cannot all enjoy an entrenched freedom to select their preferred route.

With choices that are logically incapable of co-exercise, we as a community can do nothing to deal with the problem. But there is a remedy that we can offer in the case of the farmer and the cowboy, where the contingent fact of scarcity makes co-exercise impossible. We can introduce rules that define related, usually somewhat circumscribed choices that all can exercise at once. Any advanced property system will make it possible for the cowboy and the farmer, or any similar claimants, to use land in peaceful co-existence—and to make peaceful use of any items that are designated as private or common property. The system achieves this via rules it introduces for establishing titles to ownership and the rights that ownership confers. Similarly, the rules of the road make it possible for pedestrians, cyclists, and motorists to travel at the same time, entrenching for each the free choice of destination and route so long as the destination and route are consistent with those rules.

This means that the rules introduced under a property or transport system, far from restricting freedom, may actually facilitate it. But, unsurprisingly, some rules will be better than others from the viewpoint of freedom as non-domination. We will return to this point in a moment and again in the next chapter.

WHAT CHOICES ARE CO-SATISFYING?

We saw that when a choice is not individually exercisable—when it is like mountain climbing or mastering string theory—then it cannot count as co-exercisable either. We might think on parallel lines that when a choice is not individually satisfying, as we think of it, then equally it cannot count as co-satisfying. But this would be too fast. In every society there are likely to be any number of choices that are regarded as individually unsatisfying, perhaps even regarded as individually damaging, such as the use of certain recreational drugs. But in the absence of any other objection—for example, a threat to public order—it is not clear that choices of this kind should be ruled out of the class of the basic liberties. Prohibiting access to such choices would involve using the law paternalistically to impose a community judgment on an able-minded adult (Shiffrin 2000). And being paternalistic, it would ultimately be dominating: the person would be subject to someone else's judgment or will. There is more to be said on this matter and I will return to it in the next chapter.

Thus the failure to be individually satisfying—individually satisfying, by general criteria—does not mean that a choice is not co-satisfying and not fit to count as a basic liberty. But there are many other ways in which a set of choices may fail to be co-satisfying and fail to provide a candidate for the class of basic liberties.

Consider, for example, any choices or activities in which one person is violent or aggressive to another, or perpetrates fraud on another, or even exposes others to serious risk. While everyone might pursue a harmful activity of this kind, with each exercising that choice at the same time as others, this would involve a war of all against all. And by plunging people into a war of all against all, the exercise of that choice would jeopardize everyone's satisfaction in many co-exercisable choices. Thus, if the set of basic liberties are required to be choices that are co-satisfying as well as co-exercisable, then they ought not to include the liberty of doing any such harm to others.

Or consider the choices whose availability to all would enable some to achieve a degree of power over others that fosters domination. For example, imagine a set of unrestricted liberties that might enable some to achieve a monopoly in the production of an essential grain, or to win total control over the media in the country, or simply to amass a level of wealth that makes others into effective dependents or clients. Were such choices secured as basic liberties, then the general exercise of any—in particular, its exercise by the relative winners— would be likely to deprive many of the satisfaction associated with that or other such choices. We saw earlier that there is good reason to establish rules governing the use of land and, by extension, property in general. Such rules introduce choices in the domain of ownership, exchange, and bequest that people could each exercise without coming to blows. But we now see that those same rules might enable certain individuals to gain such economic power that they are bound to dominate others— for example, in employment or legal action or competition over access to resources. The requirement to be co-satisfying would argue against establishing rules that secured or entrenched as basic liberties choices that lead to such over-empowering, destructive effects.

There is also a third set of examples where the requirement to be co-satisfying puts a serious limit on the choices that ought to be resourced and protected as basic liberties. These are choices whose exercise by a number of people—at the limit, by all—is certainly possible but is nonetheless counterproductive; it undermines the benefit that gives the choice its rationale and appeal for each. Taking an example from Herbert Hart (1973, 543), consider the case where people each have a choice of addressing a group at will—say, a local town hall meeting. It will be clearly possible for them each to address the group and to do so at the same time, so that co-exercisability is not a problem. But what if everyone addresses the group at once? Then no one is going to be heard and no one is going to be happy. In the same way, everyone may wish to own a gun, but if everyone owns a gun then, plausibly, no one is defensively better off. So, too, everyone may wish to drive into the city center, but if everyone does this at the same time then the point of driving—getting there quickly and smoothly—may be undermined.

We as a community can do much to get over some such

co-satisfaction problems. We can introduce rules under which people are given options that are close to the original, problematic options but are capable of meeting the constraint of co-satisfaction. In the case of the town hall meeting, for instance, we might deploy Robert's rules of order. These allow people to take turns in speaking, dictating a pattern under which they can each make proposals, suggest amendments to the proposals of others, and debate and vote on the various issues that arise in their discussion. As such rules might resolve the debating predicament, similar rules might resolve other problems. For example, people might be given the rule-dependent option of owning guns on condition of passing certain tests, or of using free or cheap parking facilities and taking public transport into city centers.

BACK TO THE BASIC LIBERTIES

What, then, are the sorts of choices worthy of being identified as basic liberties, being supported by common resources and being provided with public protection? What are the choices that look fit to be entrenched or secured as we apply tests of co-exercisability and co-satisfaction and seek a contemporary interpretation of the freedoms of equal republican citizenship?

The set of co-exercisable, co-satisfying choices that can and ought to be entrenched as basic liberties in any society will vary with the culture and technology and economy characteristic of that society. The choices that are co-exercisable and co-satisfying in pre-industrial societies, for example, will be very different from those that pass such constraints in advanced societies today. In an advanced society, we would naturally want security for choices such as that of looking for work by advertising your skills, by seeking information about jobs online, or by making yourself available for interview within short time spans and across quite large distances. But it would make no sense, of course, to think that similar liberties ought to be resourced and protected in societies where the relevant technologies of publicity, information, and travel were missing.

The set of choices that call for entrenchment as basic liberties are also likely to differ between quite similar developed societies. Such societies differ in cultural standards that bear on matters such as offensive speech, gun ownership, and religious diversity. It is quite likely, then, that a liberty that may seem appropriate to entrench in one context—say, the liberty to buy a gun for your private protection, or the liberty to criticize, even mock the religion of others—will not seem fit for entrenchment in another. Think of the difference between the USA and other advanced democracies in attitudes to freedom of speech, gun control, and even the separation of church and state. As between the different systems of basic liberties that are generated by such cultural variations, there is no reason to think that only a single candidate will be right from the point of view of freedom as non-domination. Culturally diverse societies may call for the entrenchment of divergent sets of basic liberties. One size may not fit all.

Apart from technological and cultural sources of variation in basic liberties, the need to establish rule-based liberties such as those associated with transport or property can generate further diversity. There may be conventions in these areas that are inimical to the equal enjoyment of freedom as non-domination, as we noted, but it is more than likely that certain rival and quite divergent sets of conventions—and sets of liberties—can serve that goal equally well. Different property systems may distinguish at different points between private property and public or communal property. And different systems may associate different rights with private ownership; in one society the ownership of land may give you mining rights, for example, while in another it may not.

The variation in acceptable sets of basic liberties should not be surprising, on a republican approach. For, as we saw in the first chapter, laws and norms according to this way of thinking constitute the freedom—the civic liberty—that people enjoy, securing them against others on appropriate fronts. They do not seek to get people as close as possible to the ideal of a natural liberty, where this is taken to be the liberty that people would enjoy in the absence of law. According to the republican way of thinking, it is not nature but society that determines the liberties we may hope to enjoy. And while we may and should require our different societies to look to republican or other ideals in fixing the range of the basic liberties—we will see something of what this entails in the coming chapters—we cannot reasonably think that there is one simple set of liberties that ought to be faithfully established in each. The basic liberties are not a natural kind. They are a kind—a set of choices—that has to be identified case by case for each culture and community.

Notwithstanding differences among various societies, however, our discussion still points us toward general categories of activity or choice in which we should expect basic liberties to be established in any society, or at least in any contemporary, relatively advanced society. Societies may differ from one another in the construal of each of those categories—for example, in determining the precise titles and rights of private ownership—but it is hard to see a justification for why a society should be entitled to neglect any one of them entirely. They count not as natural liberties that are set in stone, but rather as liberties that are universally applicable across societies, though open to variations of interpretation in each.

The following list may not be exhaustive, but it should be usefully indicative of the categories of liberty I have in mind:

- The freedom to think what you like
- The freedom to say and otherwise express what you think
- The freedom to practice the religion of your choice
- The freedom to associate with those willing to associate with you
- The freedom to own and trade under local property rules
- The freedom to change occupation and employment
- The freedom to move and settle within the society where you will
- The freedom to spend your leisure time in one or another activity

A list like this points us toward the set of choice-types in which people, assuming they are to count as equals, should enjoy freedom as non-domination. Those sets are going to assume different forms in different cultures, under different technologies, and within different patterns of commerce and exchange. But if in any society you enjoyed a form of public entrenchment that enabled you to exercise all choices in a suitable set of liberties without worrying about the goodwill of others, or the goodwill of government, then you would live up, intuitively, to the image of the *liber* or free citizen. As non-domination would give you the depth appropriate for full freedom of choice, so entrenchment in this range of choices would give you the appropriate breadth.

Would the secure enjoyment of such liberties give you access to the meaningful life that we would expect a free citizen to be able to achieve? You will have to rely on your own efforts and your own commitments, of course, actually to achieve a meaningful life. But it is hard to see how you could complain of being blocked from that achievement if you enjoyed all the resources and protections required for exercising this range of choices. If robust freedom in these choices is not enough to make a meaningful, independent life possible, what else is needed?

The following chapters should suggest that nothing more is needed, since I shall argue there that any society that provides well for such freedom will count, by intuitive criteria, as just, democratic, and sovereign. If the society entrenches each against the danger of interference from others in the domain of the basic liberties, then it will count plausibly as a just society. If this entrenchment is secured under a suitable form of control by the citizenry, then the society will count as properly democratic and the interference of government will not take from the freedom of citizens. And if the international relations among peoples guard each against the danger of domination by other states or by non-state actors, then each people will have the sovereign freedom to pursue such justice and democracy in its own case and in its own way.

PART 2

The Institutions of Freedom

Chapter 4

FREEDOM AND JUSTICE

There are two aspects to being a free citizen in a domestic polity, enjoying security in the exercise of your basic liberties. First, you must enjoy independence in relation to private individuals and associations; you must not be unprotected in relation to *dominium* or private power. And second, you must enjoy a certain independence in relation to the state; you must share in control of its doings in such a way that you are not unprotected in relation to *imperium* or public power. On the one side you must enjoy personal independence, on the other political independence.

I want to argue in this chapter that you and your fellow citizens will live in a just society to the extent that you each have the resources to exercise the basic liberties and are not subject to one another's domination in their exercise. In that case, you will enjoy the first, personal form of independence. In the next chapter, I will argue that you and your fellow citizens will enjoy the second, political form of independence to the extent that you share equally in democratic control of the state: that is, of the authorities who act in the state's name. The domestic ideals of justice and democracy, on this account, derive from freedom, where freedom is given the depth and breadth demanded by republicanism. If we look after freedom properly, then justice and democracy will look after themselves.

Returning to *A Doll's House*, if Nora is to enjoy the status of a free person in relation to other individuals, Torvald included, then she must be given equal access with her fellow citizens to a set of basic liberties that have been suitably identified, resourced, and protected by the state. And if she is to enjoy the status of a free person in relation to that state, then she must not live at the mercy of a government that she has no power to control. According to the argument of this chapter, providing Nora and her fellow citizens with a set of suitably entrenched basic liberties will mean establishing a just society. And according to the argument of the next chapter, providing her and her fellow citizens with a suitable form of shared control over government will mean establishing a properly democratic society.

Thus justice, the topic of this chapter, means justice only in the horizontal or social relations that citizens have with one another, whether within the home or workplace, in the markets or the public square. It does not involve the vertical or political relations between citizens and their government. Nor of course does it involve the lateral or international relations between one society or polity and others. Justice in this sense is usually cast as social justice, and contrasts with political justice and international justice. The issue of political justice will come up in the next chapter and the issue of international justice in the last chapter.

To begin this discussion of social justice—I will often simply say, justice—I look first at the general idea of justice, situating the republican proposal among other candidate theories. Next, I sketch the institutions that republican justice would support, covering domains of public policy-making that I describe as infrastructure, insurance, and insulation. And then, in conclusion, I explain why this approach requires only one freedom-centered principle of justice in contrast to the theory, championed by John Rawls and others, in which justice requires two principles, one bearing on equality in liberties, the other on equality in resources.

THE IDEA OF SOCIAL JUSTICE, REPUBLICAN AND OTHERWISE

Almost everyone agrees in the abstract that justice, understood in the social manner, requires what Rawls (1971, 9) describes as "a proper balance between competing claims." But who are the claimants to justice? What is the agency that is to balance their rival claims? And what are the claims that need to be balanced?

I take the citizens of the relevant society to be the claimants in justice, where the citizenry can be assumed in most contexts to include all adult, able-minded, more or less permanent residents.[39] And I take the state to be the addressee of their claims, where the state is a corporate agency—operating via the different arms of government—that assumes a unique, unchallenged authority to settle citizen claims, if necessary by recourse to coercion. What are the claims, then, that citizens are entitled to make against the state, and what would constitute a proper balance between those claims?

The state will establish a proper balance among citizen claims, however those claims are understood, only insofar as it treats citizens as equals in addressing them—only insofar as it is expressively egalitarian, as we may put the point, in dealing with its citizens. To treat people as equals in this sense does not necessarily mean giving them equal treatment (Dworkin 1978). Consider two teenage children for whose college education you are responsible as a parent. Depending on their course of study, those children may each require different levels of funding: one may opt for arts, the other for a more costly professional education. If you provide both with the money they need to enroll in their chosen coursework, you will have treated them as equals. Both will get the support they require. But since you will have provided them with different levels of funding, you will not have given them equal treatment. In the same way, when the state treats citizens as equals—say, in funding social and economic infrastructure—it may not give them equal treatment. In providing equal access to roads or water or electricity, for example, the state may have to spend much more on people who live in rural areas than on those who live in towns and cities.

The republican approach strongly supports expressive egalitarianism. In this tradition, the ideal of the free citizen requires a civic status that enables each to stand on an equal footing with others. Such a status can be established only under a state that treats all its members as equals and only under a culture in which people are each prepared to accept such treatment and to claim no special privileges. In discussing justice in this chapter, and democracy and sovereignty in the chapters that follow, I shall assume that the expressive egalitarian constraint always applies. No proposal in any of these areas can command support unless it is compatible with the principle that no one is special and that all are to count in the expressive sense as equals.

Expressive egalitarianism tells us that whatever the claims of citizens, the state will establish a proper balance among those claims—and thus achieve social justice—precisely to the extent that it treats its citizens as equals in satisfying the claims. But what are the claims in respect of which the just state should treat citizens as equals? And how much substantive equality—how much equal treatment—should the state provide in satisfaction of those claims? The central issue, in Amartya Sen's (1993) phrase, is: "Equality of what?"

There are many different responses to this question (Kymlicka 2002; Vallentyne 2007). The main competitors hold that justice requires equality in resources, in happiness, in the basic capacity for social functioning, in the mix of liberties and resources that Rawls's two principles of justice invoke—I will look briefly at these principles later—or in the many close relatives of such values. These theories are not always clear about whether it is merely expressive equality that is recommended in these dimensions or substantive equality as well (Temkin 1996). And they do not always make the distinction imposed here between issues of justice—that is, social justice—and the issues of democracy and legitimacy that come up in the next chapter (Simmons 1999). In any case, we need not dwell on them in detail. Our focal concern is with justice as it is likely to appear within a republican perspective.

Given its commitment to the value of freedom at an appropriate depth and with an appropriate breadth, a republican theory will naturally require the just state to treat citizens as equals in their claims to freedom—specifically, in their claims to freedom as that has been articulated in the first part of this book. Going on that account, the state ought to treat people as equals—it ought to be expressively egalitarian—in fostering their freedom as non-domination, on the basis of public laws and norms, within the sphere of the basic liberties. This approach is squarely in line with the republican tradition of thought, connecting with the idea that Cicero (1998, 21) voiced on freedom and equality: "Nothing can be sweeter than liberty. Yet if it isn't equal throughout, it isn't liberty at all."

But how substantively egalitarian is a republican theory of justice likely to be? On the account of freedom presented earlier, the expressively egalitarian pursuit of freedom as non-domination for all does not require a strict, substantive equality in wealth and power, although wealth and power certainly enable people to exercise choice over a wider range of options. What it calls for instead is a level of protection and resourcing for people's basic liberties—a level of entrenchment—that would enable them to count as equals in the enjoyment of freedom. I later identify this level of entrenchment as that which would enable people to pass the eyeball test: to look one another in the eye without reason for fear or deference.

While the goal of suitably resourcing and protecting people's basic liberties is distinct from that of equalizing their wealth and power, however, it is worth noting that there is a tight connection between equal freedom, in the republican sense, and material equality. Suppose that you are worse off in material respects than your neighbors. Suppose you lack some resources required for exercising the basic liberties—in skill or information, access to shelter or sustenance or income—and your neighbors enjoy an excess of such assets. Or suppose that while your legal protections against interference are barely adequate, your neighbors enjoy the benefits of private security, powerful legal representation, and good connections within the police force. In each scenario you will be less well defended against your neighbors than they are against you. And in each scenario, the state that aims to treat its citizens as equals in the enjoyment of freedom as non-domination will almost always do better in this pursuit by helping you, the worse-off party, rather than helping your richer neighbors.

There are two reasons for this (Pettit 1997b; Lovett 2001). Since you will be more exposed to domination than your neighbors, providing defenses for you is liable to reduce domination more effectively than providing extra defenses for them. And if the state were to provide extra defenses for your neighbors, it would increase the domination to which you are already exposed, enabling them to be better guarded against your efforts to defend yourself. The first consideration suggests that it will generally be underproductive to provide resources or protections for the better off rather than the worse off: it is likely to do less good. The second suggests that it will be downright counterproductive to take this line: it is likely to do more harm than good.

We are now in a position to consider the policy-making programs that a republican theory of justice is likely to support. We need to identify the programs that the state ought to implement if it is to treat its citizens as equals in satisfying their claims to freedom as non-domination. The exercise is bound to be tentative, if only because it depends on empirical assumptions that, however plausible, may be subject to challenge. Still, it should help to communicate a sense of where republican theory leads.

We can distinguish three relevant areas of policy-making for promoting people's equal enjoyment of freedom as non-domination in their relations with one another. Relying on alliteration to make the categories easy to recall, I describe the three domains as those of infrastructure, insurance, and insulation. Infrastructure encompasses the institutions presupposed to the general public's enjoyment of a meaningful range of choice, insurance to the factors essential for supporting people who fall on evil times, and insulation to defenses against the dangers occasioned by asymmetrical relationships and criminal activities.

INFRASTRUCTURE

Every theory of justice will have something to say on the infrastructure that must be provided to the citizens of a potentially just society. That infrastructure will have two aspects: institutional and material. The institutional infrastructure will have to provide for the education, training, and information available to citizens; for the legal order, public and private, that allows individuals to negotiate their relationships and resolve their problems according to established criteria and procedures; and for the investment and market conditions that facilitate the development and maintenance of a prosperous, competitive economy.

The material infrastructure will have to ensure the integrity of the territory against external danger; the provision of roads and airways and other means of transport; the coordination of access to the means of communication used by the media and among individuals; the existence, accessibility, and safety of public spaces in cities and countryside; the sustainable use of regenerating resources of food and energy—fish, timber, and the like; the responsible use of nonregenerating resources of energy such as fossil fuels; and the care of the natural and precarious environment.

The republican theory of justice, like any plausible alternative, will argue for the nurture and care of the society's infrastructure, both institutional and material, since this will affect the extent to which people can exercise and enjoy their basic liberties. But it is worth noting that the republican picture introduces a quite distinctive view of legal entitlements—in particular, the entitlements of ownership. Libertarian and other theories often suggest that the titles to property, and the rights of ownership, are written in nature's stone and determined independently of social convention. But republican theory, as we have seen, offers a different perspective and is likely to support quite different lines of policy.

The explanation goes back to a consideration, already mentioned, that in securing people against certain forms of intrusion, the laws and norms of a society make those individuals free. They constitute the freedoms that people enjoy in the way that the antibodies in your blood constitute your immunity against certain diseases. Thus, as we saw in the last chapter, each system of law establishes its own package of property titles and rights and its own account of the associated basic liberties.[40] Those titles and those rights are not established by nature; they are a product of the social order that the laws and norms put in place.[41]

In 1846, the French anarchist Pierre-Joseph Proudhon maintained famously that all property is theft, suggesting that any laws of ownership compromise people's freedom. The republican view developed in the last chapter clearly rejects that perspective, arguing that property conventions can make a basic liberty of ownership available to all. But the approach is equally opposed to the libertarian position, that since property entitlements are defined antecedently to social conventions, all taxation is theft, all regulation a form of oppression. The claim that all taxation is theft ignores the fact that taxation is an essential part of the conventions of law and norm whereby property and freedom of ownership are established in the first place (Murphy and Nagel 2004). And the claim that all regulation is a form of oppression fails to recognize that we establish most of our freedoms only by virtue of a common regulatory regime.

To make these points is not to suggest that taxation or regulation can attain any level, no matter how high, and continue to provide benefits; certain levels may be counterproductive and work against the freedom of people at large. It is to say that there are no God-given property entitlements, for example, and that each society must determine the titles and rights of private property that are to obtain there, as well as the divisions to be established between private, public, and communal property. Thus, in principle, promoting freedom as non-domination in a way that treats all as equals might argue for possibilities that libertarians are unlikely to notice or contemplate. Depending on what is required for achieving the republican conception of freedom in a changing world, the theory could support the introduction of novel conceptions of property—for example, in newly emerging areas of intellectual property or the ownership of important natural resources—and novel restrictions on how far private funds can be used for certain purposes—say, for supporting political candidates, for maintaining a private system of security, or for establishing a family financial dynasty secured under the law of trusts.

INSURANCE

After infrastructure, justice requires insurance for individuals and groups against various ills. In the case of republican justice, the ills to be insured against will involve the under-resourcing of people's basic liberties and their consequent exposure to new possibilities of domination. The insurance required may be designed to help whole populations in the event of natural catastrophes such as volcanic explosions and earthquakes, hurricanes and tornadoes, periods of drought or flooding, and epidemics. Or it may be directed at the defense of individuals against various twists of fate: temporary or permanent disability, medical need or emergency, the loss of employment, the dependency often brought about by old age, and the need for legal resources to defend against charges or to pursue complaints. Or indeed, to go to a midway possibility, it may be designed to help out one or another minority that is exposed to problems of a distinctive sort, be that minority a particular age group or refugee population or employment category. A variety of calamities can deprive people of the resources needed for the exercise of the basic liberties, leaving them unable to exercise those liberties and often exposing them to domination on the part of the more fortunate.

Right-of-center theories of justice, libertarian or liberal, tend to be dismissive of such insurance claims except, surprisingly, for claims on behalf of regional groups that suffer natural catastrophe. But a community committed to freedom as non-domination must be concerned with the insurance of individuals as well as with the insurance of localities. In order to enjoy equal freedom as non-domination, people must have sure access to shelter and nourishment, to treatment for medical need and support for disability, to representation in appearing as plaintiffs or defendants in the courts, and to support, if they need it, in their declining years. It follows that people should be publicly insured—or, if this is deemed a better alternative, be publicly required and incentivized to have private insurance—against such possibilities. They should be provided at a basic level with social security, medical security, and judicial security, whether by means of a system of social insurance, national health, and legal assistance, or by any of number of alternatives—say, the provision of a basic income for each citizen (Van Parijs 1995; Raventos 2007). They should be assured of access to what Amartya Sen (1985) and Martha Nussbaum (2006) describe as the basic capabilities for functioning in their society.

Opponents will say that private, philanthropic efforts may

better support people on these fronts, that individuals are more efficiently and effectively looked after if they have access to privately funded kitchens and shelters, for example, or to the pro bono services of philanthropic professionals like lawyers, doctors, and dentists. But assuming that such services depend on the continuing goodwill of their providers, it should be clear that from a republican point of view private philanthropy—even if it comes without problematic conditions attached—is unsatisfactory.[42] If people depend in an enduring way on the philanthropy of benefactors, then they will suffer a clear form of domination. Their expectations about the resources available will shift, and this shift will give benefactors an effective power of interference in their lives. Thus, suppose you have a continuing medical problem and depend on the pro bono services of a doctor or hospital to help you out. Once established, this dependence will put the doctor or hospital in the position of a master; you will depend for the ability to exercise various basic liberties on their not withdrawing from the relationship and leaving you in the lurch.[43]

Issues of social, medical, and judicial security have long appeared on the debating table in politics, with social democrats and progressives usually supporting such measures and libertarians and conservatives routinely opposing them. But recent developments have shown us that financial security, as we may call it, is of equal importance: that is, security against the effects that the financial markets may have on people's savings and superannuation, and on their capacity to get over crises without the philanthropy of others.

Financial security argues for familiar government guarantees in support of bank deposits, which are likely to make good economic sense anyhow, inducing confidence in the system. But it also argues for preemptive regulatory measures against excesses in the financial markets, where the huge profits available on opportunistic transactions can create unresisted temptations, induce a frenzy of competition among rival houses, and lead to a pattern of risk-taking in which the good of all is put in serious jeopardy. Regulation is not oppression, to repeat the point made earlier, and if regulation is ever desirable, it is desirable in the financial markets (Pettit 2013a).

INSULATION, SPECIAL

The third area of policy-making where justice is relevant involves the insulation of individuals against the dangers of domination by others. In this area, a natural distinction arises between two sorts of cases: one special, the other general. In the special case, people need to be insulated against the dangers associated with relationships where an asymmetry of power exists between the parties. In the general case, they need to be insulated against the dangers of crime, individual or corporate, blue-collar or white-collar.

Take the special case first. Under the republican way of thinking, people will need insulation in a variety of relationships, such as that of wife and husband, employee and employer, debtor and creditor. Standard policy-making would argue, reasonably, for equalizing the positions by imposing legal duties on the presumptively stronger party—typically, the husband, the employer, and the creditor—and reinforcing the corresponding rights of the weaker. Such rights are important but they are often frail reeds; the weaker party must trigger them and that act alone can have serious, inhibiting costs. The wife who calls in the police against an abusive husband may find herself exposed to anger and further abuse. The employees who complain to an outside inspector about working conditions may find that their boss consequently assigns them the roughest jobs.

In order to establish special insulation for these weaker parties, it is probably essential for the state to go beyond establishing suitable legal rights. It may also be necessary to screen in various options for the weaker party, as in making provision for the abused wife to take refuge in a women's home, legalizing the unionization of employees, and establishing a system of unemployment benefits. With the stronger party, it may well be necessary to screen out various options, as in providing for a court order against an abusive husband, or restricting or regulating the right of an employer to fire workers at will.[44] In addition, it will make sense to create various avenues of redress for the weaker party, as in allowing a wife to seek no-fault divorce or enabling an employee to sue for wrongful dismissal or unequal treatment in the workplace.

Are the dangers created by such asymmetries in relational power serious threats to freedom? If we think of freedom as noninterference, then the dangers are only important to the extent that actual interference is likely. Classical British liberals may not have worried about giving greater powers to husbands or employers, on the grounds, often cited at the time, that good Christian husbands would be unlikely to abuse their wives and economically rational employers unlikely to tangle with their employees. But given that we think of freedom as non-domination, any power of interference granted to a husband or employer is already a problem, even if actual interference is unlikely to occur in a given relationship. Domination materializes, after all, in virtue of the existence of such a power; it does not require the power to be exercised.

But the power may not only constitute a problem without being exercised; it may constitute a problem without even being welcomed by the power-bearer. Torvald would not cease to dominate Nora if he recognized the asymmetry in the relationship and absolutely deplored it. Given that his power derives from cultural and legal sources, it is not something he can put aside. And so Nora can be forced to depend on his goodwill, and can be deprived of freedom as non-domination, even when he does not want her to be dependent in that fashion.

Apart from the traditional relationships in which individuals need insulation against the greater power of other individuals, the relationship between individuals and corporate entities, commercial and otherwise, also introduces troubling asymmetries (Coleman 1974). Corporate entities act only via their individual members, but members play different parts and, depending on who is in the office, may play the same part at different times. Thus, they are individually shielded from scrutiny in the parts they play, and they act to an aggregate effect that may not be clearly visible to any of them (List and Pettit 2011). As a result, the artificial, composite agents they bring to life lack vulnerability and the capacity for empathy (Bakan 2004). That effect is supported by an independent factor as well. When individuals act on behalf of a corporate entity, as when they act on behalf of any principal, this can lead them to behave more callously than they would be willing to do in their own name; it can make such callous behavior less shameful and embarrassing than it would otherwise be (Brennan and Pettit 2004).

Examples of corporate domination are commonplace. Think of the case of someone abused by a priest in childhood who contemplates bringing a complaint against a powerful church. Think of the case of small entrepreneurs who are held to ransom by the primary or secondary picketing of a powerful trade union that can put them out of business. Or think, even more saliently, of those with a claim for damages—say, damages resulting from an oil spillage or explosion—against a large corporation. The prospect for domination in each of these cases is enormous. Compared with individual human beings, corporate organizations generally have an indefinite time-horizon, an endless fund of indifference to life's anxieties, and a more or less bottomless purse. They represent a new and powerful challenge to individual freedom.

How should we deal with the challenge posed by corporate domination? I have no easy solution to offer, especially since legal systems worldwide have been progressively increasing the rights of organizations, in particular commercial corporations, over the last couple of centuries. Governments have competed with one another to attract multinational companies to their shores by giving them ever more rights and powers, apparently oblivious of the impact of corporate power on the freedom of their citizens.[45]

Perhaps the best hope of empowering individuals in the face of corporate titans is to establish avenues for bringing complaints and charges in public forums—especially in the criminal courts—where indictment carries a great penalty for the reputation of the offending body. Corporate organizations may be able to cope with financial fines, but they all shrink in horror from bad publicity. Bad publicity can deprive churches of their congregations, unions of their support in the labor movement, and corporations of their very lifeblood: the customers who buy their products.

We have looked at troublesome asymmetries of power that arise as a result of more or less personal relationships in the family or workplace, and as a result of the relationships between individuals and corporate bodies. Without going into the issue in detail, it is also worth mentioning that in any population there are often going to be special groups whose members are systematically vulnerable in their relationships to those in the relative mainstream. Those groups may be defined by age or employment, ethnicity or religion, gender or sexual orientation, language or migrant status, The measures required for protecting individuals in this category are as various as the sorts of problems that arise in the other relationships; it is particularly hard to generalize. But we should at least register the case, within republican theory, for seeking special insulation for the members of such vulnerable groups as well as for people in the other categories.

INSULATION, GENERAL

Insulation is also required to guard against dangers to which people in general are exposed, not just those in special relationships. The exemplars of such general dangers are acts that deserve by almost all lights to be criminalized: for example, murder, assault, rape, fraud, and theft. There are many issues here and I can only gesture at them in the most cursory way, sketching out the theory of criminal justice that a republican philosophy would support (Braithwaite and Pettit 1990; Pettit 1997a; 2014a).

Paradigm crimes of the kind mentioned involve a serious, dominating form of interference in the domain of the basic liberties and, plausibly, republican theory will call for the criminalization of such acts and indeed of any acts of a similar dominating character. But the theory is also likely to support the criminalization of acts that make such dominating interference more likely, even if they are not dominating in themselves: for example, acts of organizing with the intent to commit a crime, acts of inciting others to commit crime, or acts of seeking to undermine the criminal justice system itself. At least, the theory will support criminalization in these categories insofar as that is not counterproductive or useless. Thus, it would be useless to criminalize routine deception or infidelity if the social norms associated with law can keep them within reasonable bounds. And it would be counterproductive to do so if investing the state with the power to police such an activity—here I anticipate themes from the next chapter—held out a greater prospect of domination than the activity itself.

The criminalization of different activities involves the introduction of deterrent penalties—jail time, fines, community service—for offenders as distinct, for example, from offering rewards to non-offenders. More specifically, it involves the introduction of deterrent penalties on the presumptive grounds that the community condemns the acts in question (Duff 2001); the penalties introduced are not simply costs that you can treat as payment for being allowed to perform those acts. The criminalization of certain activities aims to protect individuals from offenses against their basic liberties, or from acts that make offenses likely, reinforcing people in their status as equally free with the best (Kelly 2009). When offenses have been committed, therefore, this aim commits the state to seek to apprehend the offenders and to impose the associated penalties. This both gives credibility to the protective scheme in general and reaffirms the protected status of the victim and/or those who are vulnerable in the same way: those for whom the victim exemplifies the dangers to which they are subject.

What form should the criminal justice system assume, under a republican theory? In dealing with this question, we primarily have to consider the requirements for protecting potential victims against criminal abuse. But, anticipating the next chapter, we cannot avoid considering also the danger of investing the state with excessive power in the area of criminal justice. Let the agents of the state be given great powers in this domain and it may prove difficult or impossible to impose effective democratic control over how they exercise those powers; it may be hard to guard against domination from above.

Given the oppressive, potentially dominating role of the state in the area of criminal justice, republican theory would argue in the first place for criminalizing only serious offenses. It would oppose the tendency to give the standing of criminal laws to public regulations governing matters like speeding, loitering, and littering (Husak 2008). And it would look for a pattern of policing and surveillance, prosecution, adjudication, and sentencing in which the agents of the state are severely restricted in the initiatives they can take and are forced to bear the onus of establishing the guilt of offenders.

Perhaps the most important requirement of such a criminal justice system is to protect against the possibility of an innocent person being punished. If agents of the state were entitled to impose sanctions independently of stringent tests of culpability, then they would possess an extraordinary degree of dominating power. They would not face sufficiently high barriers against scapegoating the innocent or singling out certain offenders for exemplary punishment. They would have enough power to intimidate whole sectors of the community.

What sorts of sentences or penalties would the theory support? Ideally, any penalty should reaffirm the status of the victim, help to provide whatever compensation is plausible, and reassure the community that the offense has not raised the likelihood of such offenses in general. The victims of assault or theft—and the families of murder victims—ought to be able to feel that what was done to them has been recognized as a wrong by the community in general and, ideally, by the offender. Equally, they ought to be provided with some measure of restitution or reparation. And they and members of the community as a whole ought to be able to think that their prospects of suffering similar crimes are no greater, in the wake of the offender's conviction, than they were before the offense.

This approach to criminalization would allow for the possibility of mercy—say, if an offender without a record displays credible repentance and is judged, for whatever reason, not to be a threat to the community. And where mercy is denied, the approach would look for penalties that do not lock out offenders from the possibility of being reincorporated in the society as full and free citizens. This argues for a presumption in favor of more parsimonious penalties, supporting community service orders over fines, fines over imprisonment, and imprisonment over capital punishment. The criminal system should be designed to provide for the restoration of offenders as well as victims to the status of republican citizenship and freedom.

While rival theories say little or nothing about the practice of criminal justice, the republican approach makes a case for the radical reform of contemporary criminal justice systems, as even these brief comments should indicate (Braithwaite and Pettit 1990; Pettit 1997a; 2014a). This is an area of more or less salient and recurring abuse. The abuses are evident in the increasing numbers of citizens imprisoned across the world, the longer and longer terms to which they are often sentenced, the humiliation and assault to which prisoners are subject, and the failure in most systems to do anything serious in the way of reincorporating offenders into the community. Republican theory supports a radical overhaul of the criminal justice system, seeking to replace it with practices that would better promote people's general security in the exercise of their basic liberties.

But we should add one final, cautionary note. The proposals canvassed here on matters of criminal justice presuppose conditions in which relatively few actions are criminalized, relatively few crimes are committed, and relatively few offenders have to be charged, brought to trial, and punished; such conditions are necessary to allow a proper hearing to be given to each particular case. But these conditions often fail in the real world. Police are overwhelmed by the challenges they face, public prosecutors have to deal with excessive workloads, defendants are not assured of proper legal representation, the courts find questionable ways of fast-tracking their processes, and the convicted become society's rejects, dumped in overcrowded prisons or stigmatized forever in the wider community. These shortfalls from the conditions presupposed in our theory are so dramatic that they may argue for modifications to the proposals made and adjustments to the practices described. In imperfect situations, it may often be better not to try to replicate the arrangements that are abstractly most appealing, but rather to consider institutional innovations (Vermeule 2011).

It may make very good sense, in this spirit, to look for radical variations on the sort of criminal justice system we have been envisaging. We might try to supplement the criminal justice system, for example, with novel programs of restorative justice in which certain offenders can plead guilty and avoid normal judicial process. Under such a program, the admitted offender enters a conference with the victim, in the presence of a number of associates chosen by each, to determine what the offender should do to make up for the offense (Strang and Braithwaite 2000; Braithwaite 2002; Johnstone 2003). While I have not been able to explore the possibility here, restorative justice programs may well promise in real-world circumstances—and, indeed, in more ideal conditions too (Braithwaite and

Parker 1999)—to serve criminal justice better than anything I have space to consider.

Is there any serious prospect of being able to humanize criminal justice systems, bringing them more into line with the sorts of desiderata signaled? One major problem, as things stand, is that many democracies leave issues of criminal justice under the immediate control of elected officials rather than putting them at arm's length from the theater of popular politics (Pettit 2002a).[46] That means that politicians have to respond—usually in a sound bite or headline—to the anger and emotion that any serious crime understandably elicits. Therefore, they often have to make criminal justice policy in an atmosphere where anything less than a display of shock and horror, and a call for extreme measures, is bound to seem heartless and inadequate. I return to this point in the next chapter, suggesting that in the area of criminal justice, as in some other domains of policy-making, democracy may be better served by institutions that are designed primarily to register and reflect stable community standards, not to channel case-by-case responses.

JUSTICE AND THE EYEBALL TEST

This brief and tentative sketch should give a general idea of the institutions of justice that the republican theory ought to support in matters of infrastructure, insurance, and insulation. But we can hardly conclude the sketch without asking about the level of provision that is required in these areas. How much in the way of infrastructure, insurance, and insulation ought to be made available in order for people to enjoy freedom as non-domination? What counts as enough to ensure the result sought in the theory?

Under the republican theory of social justice, the laws and norms of the society should identify a suitable set of basic liberties, and then resource and protect them up to the point where, intuitively, no more calls to be done: this is the point at which people count as equals in the enjoyment of freedom as non-domination. While there may be slack enough to allow differences in private resources and protections, all must equally enjoy an adequate level of entrenchment in the exercise of those liberties.

But what level of resourcing and protection is to count as adequate? What measure of entrenchment is going to count as enough? We have to be able to give an answer to this question, however approximate, since otherwise there may be no end to the resources and protections that might be demanded in the name of republican justice. The ideal might begin to look like an inherently unsatisfiable demand, something not appropriate for the guidance of real-world policy-making.

It is at this point that the eyeball test mentioned in the prologue becomes relevant. That test is grounded in the image of the free citizen—the *liber* or freeman—of republican tradition. It says that people will be adequately resourced and protected in the exercise of their basic liberties to the extent that, absent excessive timidity or the like, they are enabled by the most demanding local standards to look one another in the eye without reason for fear or deference. They are able to walk tall, as we put it, enjoying a communal form of recognition that they are each more or less proof against the interference of others; in that sense, they command the respect of all.

The eyeball test makes justice easier rather than harder to achieve. It means that justice is compatible with failures of personal affirmation that are due to timidity or similar failures. And in allowing for a degree of material slack, it means that social justice may be compatible with certain differences in wealth and power. Some differences may jeopardize the freedom as non-domination of the less well-off, as we mentioned in the last chapter, but many differences can still allow richer and poorer to be able to look one another in the eye without reason for fear or deference. The eyeball test allows for departures from substantive equality in such material matters, directing us instead to the importance of equality in the interactions that people are capable of enjoying with one another.[47]

While the eyeball test puts the ideal of republican justice within feasible reach, however, not mandating impossible levels of personal assurance or material equality, it ought to appeal to the most idealistic minds. It is a commonplace that a higher performance in any domain tends to generate higher expectations and standards; as a community becomes generally more caring or polite or peaceable, we will raise our expectations and standards of care, politesse, and peacefulness (Brennan and Pettit 2004). Suppose, then, that a society does better and better at achieving what counts at any time as enough to enable people to satisfy the eyeball test. As it does better in that respect, the local standards of what the test requires are likely to rise in tandem; as the society gives better protection to someone like Nora, for example, the standards for what counts as adequate protection are likely to lift in consequence. So while we embrace the ideal in any period as a feasible and useful guide to policy, we need not think that it points us to a steady state—just around the corner, as it were— where there is nothing else to be done. The ideal is inherently dynamic and developmental.

I have been suggesting that the eyeball test will give us a rough-and-ready guide to how much is required for the resourcing and protection of the basic liberties. But I should add that it is likely to argue for different degrees of resourcing and protection in regard to different liberties. Not all liberties will call for protection in criminal law, which may be counterproductive; many will be better protected by social norms alone. And while some basic liberties may call urgently for resourcing, as we have seen, whether in providing for infrastructure or insurance, others do not. Consider, for example, the liberty to use recreational drugs, assuming that usage may involve personal risk but is not a public danger. The fact that recreational drug use involves personal risk argues against providing resources to make it generally accessible, even while concerns about domination, as we saw in the last chapter, argue for protecting people's liberty in this area. Indeed, there may even be reason to impose a heavy tax on drugs—to resource drug usage negatively, so to speak—in order to signal the personal risk involved and to encourage a general reluctance among the population to run that risk.[48]

One final question: As we saw in the second chapter, the basic liberties to be entrenched up to the level where people pass the eyeball test are not of a natural kind, and even similar societies may vary in how they define them in law and norm. Is there any way in which we might identify the best set or sets of basic liberties for a given society? I have ignored that question until now, because the obvious suggestion is that at this point too we should fall back on the eyeball test. Whatever basic liberties are established, they should be identified as well as entrenched in the manner that best facilitates people's meeting the eyeball test and enjoying the full and equal status of republican citizenship.

THE BOTTOM LINE

This sketch of the republican theory of justice would be incomplete without a comparison with rival approaches and some consideration of the novelty inherent in the practical reforms for which it calls. Every normative theory, whether in the social, democratic, or international area, is characterized by two elements: first, the base from which it argues for its recommendations, and second, the substance of the policies that it supports. The republican theory of justice—and, indeed, the republican theory of democracy and sovereignty—argues from a minimal base, viz. the requirements of freedom alone, but still manages to support a substantive and revisionary set of policies (Cohen 2004).

The minimalist base puts the theory in stark opposition to the various programs that political parties support. It offers a clear vision of what law and government should be doing in matters of social justice—promoting people's equal enjoyment of freedom as non-domination—which makes a refreshing contrast to the jumbled, opportunistic shopping lists produced by social democratic and liberal democratic parties at the polls. The republican approach scores in simplicity, memorability, and the capacity to orientate planning over the potpourri of proposals that even the most stable party program represents.

But its minimalism also marks off the republican theory from some of the best-known philosophies in the area of social justice. Thus, while the approach invokes a single freedom-centered principle in order to elaborate the demands of justice, the alternative championed by John Rawls (1971; 1993; 2001) invokes two distinct principles: one focused on liberty, the other on socioeconomic equality.[49] To quote from one of his presentations of that theory:

a. Each person has an equal right to a fully adequate scheme of equal basic liberties which is compatible with a similar scheme of liberties for all.

b. Social and economic inequalities are to satisfy two conditions. First, they must be attached to offices and positions open to all under conditions of fair equality of opportunity; and second, they must be to the greatest benefit of the least advantaged members of society. (Rawls 1993, 291)

How can the republican theory of justice endorse a principle of freedom of a kind with the first of Rawls's principles while neglecting the second?[50] There are two considerations to mention in response. First, the freedom targeted in republican justice is, as we know, a freedom that presupposes the resources required to make it effective, whereas Rawls's theory is built around a weaker conception of freedom's demands—one under which people's equal freedom, as prescribed in the first principle, does not require them to have the resources needed to exercise and value that freedom (Rawls 1971, 204–5). And second, the freedom promoted in republican theory requires protections to guard against any power of interference on the part of others, not just to make interference by others unlikely. Rawls thinks that there is a need to guard against interference only insofar as it is a probable prospect, and so he weakens the case for robust insurance and insulation; he suggests that to depend on the goodwill of someone who is unlikely to turn nasty—and someone, therefore, who is not subjected to heavy sanctions—is not lamentable in itself (Rawls 1971, 240).

For these reasons, it should be no surprise that while Rawls needs to supplement the principle ordaining equality in freedom with a principle requiring that socioeconomic resources should be more or less equal, republican theory does not have to look beyond the demands of freedom alone. The theory interprets freedom in a richer manner than Rawls and so, unsurprisingly, it is capable of building a suitable account of social justice on the requirements of freedom and freedom alone; it does not have to introduce an independent concern with socioeconomic equality.

Not only does the republican theory of justice have a simpler and more unified base than rival approaches, popular and philosophical alike, it also supports a substantive, more appealing set of demands and policies. The proposals that are likely to be supported by the theory, as should be clear by now, often coincide individually with proposals that have cropped up in popular politics and philosophical theory; it would be amazing if they did not. But as a bunch, they are more demanding and more coherent than most competitors.

The demanding character of the policies supported in the republican theory of justice can be seen in some of its more salient features and more likely recommendations:

- The theory entails that taxation is an essential aspect of any property system, distinguishing it sharply from any sort of theft, and thereby sidelines the antitax presumption that paralyzes practical politics in many societies today.
- While it looks for equality of status, not strict material equality, it acknowledges the connection between the two and would certainly indict the recent emergence of a mega-wealthy elite with powers of avoiding taxation, influencing government, and creating oligarchies.
- Recognizing the need for the state to maintain a material and institutional environment fit to facilitate freedom, it would focus on maintaining a sustainable natural

environment—perhaps our most urgent challenge today (Broome 2012)—as well as a suitable urban and institutional environment.

- Dependency on the goodwill of others for avoiding ill-treatment already undermines republican freedom, even in the absence of ill-treatment, and so the theory would look for a legal and economic order in which exposure to possible abuse, and not just the experience of abuse, is minimized.

- Thus it would argue for a public system of social, medical, and judicial security—and a form of financial security—for everyone; in particular, it would reject the idea that private philanthropy can provide all that is required on these fronts.

- It would argue equally for publicly providing a raft of rights and powers—and publicly facilitating the social movements that can give them effect—that would enable a vulnerable domestic partner not to have to live in fear of or deference to the other.

- On the same grounds, the theory would support constraints within workplace relations that deny an employer the right to fire without cause, imposing something like a requirement to defend an appeal against dismissal in an agreed forum.

- While recognizing the role of unions in protecting employees, it would defend constraints on how far a union can resort to strike action, whether in primary or secondary picketing of a firm; for example, it might require prior recourse to arbitration of the grievance.

- Since corporations have enormous legal, financial, and political power, the theory would foster initiatives for limiting their capacity to counter individual civil claims against them by dragging out cases in the courts and thereby imposing heavy costs on individual plaintiffs.

• While the theory would argue for the importance of the criminal justice system, it would support severe limits on the actions that the state can indict, on the measures of surveillance, prosecution, and conviction that it can employ, and on the sorts of penalties, ranging from community service to fines to imprisonment, that it can impose.

• Where real-world constraints put limits on the feasibility of running a normal criminal justice system, the theory would support restorative justice programs under which certain categories of offenders who admit their guilt are allowed to enter a conference with their victims, or their victims' families, to determine what they need to do by way of rectifying their offense.

• Finally, the theory would argue that corporate bodies like corporations or churches, and not just individual agents, should be capable of being indicted in the criminal justice system; the ignominy attached to a criminal sentence may hold out the best hope of keeping such titans in check.

These points all bear on justice for adult, able-minded individuals, since we have been abstracting from the needs of children and those who are cognitively impaired. Even in that restricted area, they are meant to be illustrative, not exhaustive. But still, they should serve to display and demonstrate the kind of recommendations that a republican theory of justice would be likely to support.

How appealing are those recommendations? How plausible are they in comparison with standard party political platforms and with existing competitors on the philosophical scene? The question takes us back to John Rawls's (1971) test of reflective equilibrium, which we mentioned in chapter 2. The idea is to see how far the judgments and policies on social justice that republican theory supports prove on reflection to be plausible—in particular, to see how far they compare in plausibility with alternatives.

The demands made by republican theory are more extensive and coherent, and indeed individually more compelling, than the run-of-the-mill programs that political parties provide. Perhaps there is no surprise there, since parties are as much concerned with winning over the median voter as they are with elaborating abstractly attractive sets of policies. But the republican demands also compare favorably with the sorts of policies that rival philosophical approaches support. They certainly compare well with right-of-center programs that would systematically ignore many of the ailments identified in our list. But they also compare well with the left-of-center policies embraced by Rawls and others.

In one respect the demands are not as extensive as Rawls's, for his second principle of justice would look for material equality up to the point, possibly hard to reach, where allowing a degree of relative inequality would improve the absolute returns to the worst-off position. Nor are the republican demands as extensive in this way as those of even more egalitarian theories that seek, for example, the elimination of all the effects of brute luck on people's fortunes.[51] But these radical competitors are downright implausible.

Their radicalism is excessive in one way, selective in another. In arguing in radical vein for something close to material equality, the competing theories seem like moral fantasies: manuals for how God ought to have ordained the order of things rather than real-world recommendations for what the state should do in regulating the affairs of its citizens. And in concentrating on such egalitarian proposals, they are too selective; they pay little or no attention to other areas of policy that any theory of justice ought to be concerned with. Thus, they have little or nothing to say about mundane but pressing issues like those raised by dependency in asymmetrical relationships, by the horrors of most existing criminal justice systems, or by the growth and dominance of national and multinational corporations.

Judged by the standard of reflective equilibrium, then, the republican theory of justice does better than these or any other alternatives. The recommendations it supports are challenging yet sensible proposals and would go a long way toward making any regime into an intuitively just society. If the republican theory of justice is to be judged by the character of the proposals it supports, as reflective equilibrium requires, then there are few grounds for being concerned about its credentials.

Chapter 5

FREEDOM AND DEMOCRACY

Every year a number of reports surface that attempt to rank the world's most livable cities. In arriving at their rankings, the reports consider the services available in each city, the cost of living, the natural surroundings, and other amenities. But the reports do not generally factor in the residents' level of control over how things are done in government. They consider how residents benefit from what a given city offers, but they usually ignore whether and to what extent residents have a role as the makers and shapers of the arrangements under which they live. The reports treat residents as consumers of cities, we might say, not properly as citizens.

In its discussions of different social orders, political philosophy sometimes treats people as consumers and ignores their role as citizens. It weighs the rival attractions of living as the beneficiaries (or consumers) of rival structures or arrangements. Structures in which material equality is the primary goal are considered against alternatives in which libertarian freedom or utilitarian happiness, or a mix of such goods, is all that matters. But this type of discussion ignores or downplays the significance for inhabitants of how far they share in control of the different orders under consideration—how far they figure, not as consumers of the arrangements associated with one or another social order, but as the citizens whose duty and right it is to determine the shape of those arrangements. John Rawls (1971) himself may encourage this neglect when he thrusts impartiality upon us by asking us to consider what social structure we would choose if we were ignorant of how we personally would fare under any arrangement chosen.[52]

A republican approach rectifies this neglect of the citizens' share of control in the social order. The conception of freedom as non-domination clearly puts two distinct domestic issues on the table. The first, as we have seen, concerns how to resource and protect people against the possibility of domination by private power or *dominium*, thereby promoting their satisfaction as the consumers of the social order under which they live. And the second concerns how to ensure that the public power or *imperium* through which this resourcing and protection is provided is itself not dominating—how to ensure that citizens can shape and reshape the order imposed.

The answer to the first question, as we saw in the last chapter, gives us a republican theory of justice, prescribing institutions under which people would enjoy freedom in the same fundamental choices, on the same public basis. The answer to the second question, as we shall see in this chapter, leads us to a republican theory of democracy. As few if any societies measure up to the republican standard of justice, so we shall see that few if any measure up to the republican standard of democracy. While each standard represents an attainable ideal, it is an ideal that societies generally fail to reach.

THE ROLE OF DEMOCRACY
IN REPUBLICAN THOUGHT

In the last chapter, I began from the assumption that justice should be provided by the public power of a coercive state. Having seen what justice actually requires, we can now see why this is so. It might be possible to establish a social order, without the help of the state, on the basis of spontaneously appearing social norms—regularities, as we described them earlier, sustained by the universal and manifest expectation that compliance will attract approval and/or deviance disapproval.[53] But it is hard to see how such a spontaneous, state-independent order could identify basic liberties reliably and maintain the equal resourcing and protection of those liberties that is required by social justice. It appears to be inevitable that wealth and power will accumulate in fewer and fewer hands in the absence of a coercive state. As by an "iron law," as one recent political historian writes, "the rich tend to get richer, in the absence of state intervention" (Fukuyama 2011, 368).[54]

If protection against private domination requires a coercive state, then the specter of public power looms large. For the coercive state is essentially an interfering state: it intrudes in the lives of its citizens by enacting laws, levying taxes, and imposing penalties. The core idea in the republican response to the challenge posed by such power is that nevertheless this interference by the state need not be a threat to people's freedom. That is, it need not dominate them.

State interference will not be dominating, so the thinking goes, so long as it can be subjected to the effective, equally shared control of the people. This requires more than making the state's decisions with a simple majority, since a majority-based system might marginalize some individuals and effectively deny them a share in control. It requires giving people an equally shared form of control and, as we shall see, a majoritarian system does not guarantee equal sharing.

But why should you or anyone else be happy about sharing equally with others in exercising control over the state? Why should you not hold out for a more unilateral form of power—say, the power that would go with having a veto over anything the state proposes to do? Giving everyone a veto would be inconsistent with having an effective state and so inconsistent with protection against private power. And, in any case, if you are prepared to be treated as equal with others, as expressive egalitarianism requires—if you do not claim a special position for yourself—then you must be willing to settle for sharing equally in control over the state.

Why would a regime of equal, effective control over the state make the interference of the state non-dominating? The idea is that it would be a form of interference that you and others in your society control, and that it would not involve the imposition of an alien will. Think of the example mentioned earlier, in which I hold your passport under instructions not to hand it back at less than a week's notice. While I may interfere with you in refusing to hand it back, thereby blocking the trip you want to make this weekend, the interference I practice is arguably non-dominating; it reflects your enduring, authorized will and not an arbitrary wish on my own part. The proposal to be considered here is that in the same way, if you and your fellow citizens share equally in controlling the interference of the state in your lives—if you control the laws it imposes, for example, and the taxes it levies—then you will not be dominated by the state. Its interference will not reflect any subjection to an alien will.

Consistent with etymology and ordinary usage, we can define a democracy as a system under which individuals share—and in particular, share equally[55]—in the *kratos* or control of the *demos* or people over government (Ober 2008). In its emphasis on the need to guard against public domination, republican theory offers a job specification for democracy. Democracy's entire reason for being, under this specification, is to guard against the domination of the state. And democratic theory exists to identify the institutions whereby that goal might be advanced. Democracy ought to enable people to enjoy freedom in relation to public power, as justice enables them to enjoy freedom in relation to private power. Its role should be to implement the requirements of living as a *liber* or free citizen in what we called the vertical dimension, as the role of justice is to implement its requirements in the horizontal.[56]

This brief account of the role of democracy in republican thought leaves us with two prominent questions.

1. *Would full democratic control of government, were it achievable, really enable people to enjoy freedom in their vertical relations to the state?*

I shall argue that it would. That raises a second question, which will concern us in the greater part of the chapter.

2. *Are there institutions that might enable people to achieve or approximate such full democratic control of government?*

I shall argue that there are and that while many are foreshadowed in existing democracies, their proper realization has so far proved elusive.

Before turning to our two questions, it may be useful to comment briefly on the practical significance of deciding that our society is just or unjust, democratic or undemocratic. To the extent that the laws imposed in a social order are just, we will have a strong moral reason to obey them, albeit one that might be overridden in certain circumstances. This reason is stronger, in particular, than the second-grade reason we may have to obey some unjust laws, that they serve a useful purpose in coordinating people's behavior (Raz 1986).

To the extent that the laws are imposed democratically—shaped under the effective, equally shared control of the people—we will have an equally strong moral reason, if we oppose them, to oppose them only within the system: that is, only in a way that acknowledges that there is no cause for regime change. And, in parallel to the justice case, this is stronger in particular than the second-grade reason we may have not to oppose even undemocratically imposed laws, that doing so is more likely than more violent alternatives to lead toward democracy at an acceptable cost. The strength of the stronger reason provided is hard to exaggerate. If the system under which you live is genuinely democratic—if it is subject to equal control by the citizenry—then opposing its laws outside the system, say by subversion or rebellion, would amount to assuming that you are special and so to rejecting expressive egalitarianism.

A democratic government is almost certain to impose some laws that you consider unjust or otherwise objectionable; with varying conceptions of justice, after all, we are each bound to consider some laws as unjust (Nagel 1987).[57] The fact that the government is democratic in the republican sense, however—or the fact that it scores acceptably on this metric—will argue conclusively for contesting the laws within the system and renouncing subversive or violent resistance. Contesting the laws within the system may mean appealing to your representative, to an ombudsman, or to the courts, or taking to the media or the streets. At the limit, it may also involve civil disobedience: that is, openly violating the law, inviting arrest, and accepting punishment in expression of your opposition to something done or proposed by government. Civil disobedience operates within the system to the extent that it involves accepting the right of the government to penalize the disobedience to the law that it involves.[58]

Question 1: Would full democratic control suffice for freedom?

Imagine for a moment that you are lucky enough to live in a society where you share equally in an effective system of popular or civic control over government and over the laws and other measures that government introduces. Imagine you live in a society that by republican standards constitutes a full and satisfactory democracy, whatever institutions might serve to realize it. Would this society silence every complaint of a freedom-based kind about how you are treated by the state? Would it leave nothing that you might reasonably protest about in the name of your individual freedom?

The democracy envisaged ought certainly to silence any complaints you might have about the genesis of the laws introduced, the policies implemented, and the particular decisions taken by the various branches of government and state. After all, if those laws, policies, and decisions conform to the terms that the people impose on government—we shall see later what exactly this might mean—and if you play an equal part with others in imposing those terms, then it is hard to see how you could object to the way they are generated. You could only

object if you considered yourself special and were unhappy
with merely playing the same part as others in the exercise of
popular control. And such an objection, violating the spirit of
expressive equality, would scarcely deserve a hearing.

But apart from complaints about the genesis of particular
government acts, you might feel entitled to make other complaints, even under a well-functioning democracy. You might
complain that you were never given a choice about whether
to live with others in political society. Or you might complain
that you were never given a choice about whether to live in this
particular society rather than any other. Or you might complain that from your earliest adult days the law was coercively
imposed on you, without consultation, under threat of punishment for noncompliance; you were not given the opportunity
to agree voluntarily to obey the law. Even if the state operates
on the basis of a democratic system of effective control in which
you equally share, still it is bound to constrain you in these various ways. It does not give you the option of living out of society,
political or otherwise; it does not give you the option of living in
another political society; and it does not give you the option of
not being coercively required to conform to the law.

In the tradition of republican thought, people were generally
indifferent to these sorts of complaints, taking it for granted that
human beings are social creatures, that it is chance that decides
on where they are born and live, not anyone's dictate, and that
legal coercion is part and parcel of social life. For them, the
only real question was whether government abuses its *imperium*,
whether it is arbitrary and dominating in the way it determines
law and policy. But that indifference came to be challenged
in the sixteenth and seventeenth centuries, perhaps under the
stimulus of discovering the New World. Many thinkers began
at this time to support two theses:[59] first, that political society

was actually formed, or at least ought to have been formed, on the basis of a free contract between individual agents in a state of nature; and second, that a political society counts as legitimate, and properly democratic, only insofar as its people at least implicitly consent to belonging to it: that is, consent to belonging to political society in general, and to this society in particular, living on terms that give the state coercive power over them. These two theses define what is often described as political contractarianism.[60]

Does the fact that you have no option about living in political society with others, or no option about living in this society in particular, or no option about living under coercively imposed law, mean that regardless of how democratic it proves to be, the state denies you the proper enjoyment of freedom as non-domination? Does it mean that the state is inescapably an agent of domination in your life? I reject the contractarian assumptions and answer that it does not.

Why do you have to live in political society? Not because your state condemns you to a political existence, as if it had a choice about whether or not to do so. Rather, because there is no effectively stateless zone left on earth and because even if your state relinquished its patch of land, the territory would be inevitably seized by other states. You are condemned to life in a polity as a matter of historical necessity, in other words, not by the will of your state or indeed of any other state.

Does the state dominate you nonetheless insofar as it fails to abdicate and is the force that actually imposes a political existence? No it does not. To recall a point from chapter 2, the preference it displays in imposing such an existence is not formed on a voluntary basis and does not express a discretionary attitude toward you and your fellow citizens. It is constrained by the expectation, grounded in local standards, that as a state it will guard you and your fellow citizens against domination by other agencies. Given the threat from other states, then—foreign and inevitably dominating states—it is politically constrained to stay in place and stop them from invading the territory. Those who act for the state can present themselves as having no choice in the matter. Like Luther, they can say: Here we stand, we can do no other.

Why, to move to the second issue, do you have to live in this particular polity rather than any other? Not, we may assume, because your own country forbids you to emigrate; if it did, then it would surely dominate you. Rather, because other countries keep you out, putting a limit on the number of immigrants they take and sticking to one or another procedure for determining who gets in. Do these others states dominate you in such a case, even if your own state does not? Not necessarily, because under received standards they are functionally committed, on pain of not surviving as feasible protectors of their own citizens, to stick to a procedure for limiting immigrants. And that commitment constrains their discretion to act on the basis of the goodwill or the ill will they may happen to bear you. Again, they do not have a voluntary preference in how they treat you.

Why, finally, do you have to live under a coercively imposed law rather than being asked if you want to make a voluntary commitment to obey the law? There are two considerations relevant to the answer. First, that by all accounts some citizens have to be coerced to obey the law, both to ensure compliance and to assure others of their compliance. And second, that the state is bound to treat all citizens as equals, imposing coercion on all if it imposes coercion on any. No state could claim to treat its members as equals—as, presumptively, states are expected to do under accepted standards—if it tried to enforce a distinction between coerced and uncoerced citizens. The state is bound by this functional constraint, then, to be universally coercive; it does not have a voluntary preference in the matter of how to treat you in particular.

The three effects cited do not imply, then, that the state inevitably subjects you to an alien, unconstrained will. The state may well invade your freedom, and may well prove to be undemocratic, in the laws or other measures it chooses to impose. But it does not invade your freedom, and does not count as undemocratic, just by virtue of existing. You may rail at the restrictions associated with having to live a political existence, to live in one or another country, and to live under coercive rule. But those restrictions reflect the constraints that accepted standards impose on states; they do not derive from the exercise of voluntary preferences on the part of your state, or indeed of any other. You may long for a world that is free of coercive states, of course, and lament the developments of the last couple of thousand years (Fukuyama 2011). But this is like hankering after a world in which you are not subject to the force of gravity. It does not reflect any justifiable complaint against the state, or at least any complaint that might be justified in terms of republican freedom.[61]

We saw earlier that I do not dominate you when, in the example presented, I deny you access to your passport. In that case, two independent conditions hold, each with its own importance. First, you can set aside the arrangement allowing my refusal and interference, at least on a week's notice, so that the existence of the arrangement is not itself dominating. And, second, the interference licensed is subject to your continuing control—you could change the terms, for example by requiring only twenty-four hours' notice—so that the exercise of the power allowed by the arrangement is no more dominating than the existence of the arrangement.[62]

The situation we are now considering is similar in one way to this scenario but different in another. The existence of the arrangement under which you have to live in a particular political society, subject like others to coercive law, is not one that you can set aside; that is where the difference comes. But the existence of the arrangement still does not involve domination. The arrangement is the result of the state-bound history of the planet, and the complex of constraints to which every state is subject; it is not imposed at the voluntary will of the state or any other agency. And so for that very distinctive reason the existence of the arrangement, like the existence of the arrangement whereby I hold your passport, is not dominating as such. Like gravity, it is certainly restrictive, but it does not impose the voluntary preference of another agent or agency.

The question in this political case, then, is whether the exercise of government power allowed under the arrangement is or is not dominating. And here, by analogy with the passport case, the interference will be undominating to the extent that it is subject to the effective control of interferees. State interference will be subject in a suitable way to the control of the interferees—that is, you and other citizens—insofar as you share equally in imposing that control. Forced by historical fact to live in a political community, you will escape domination insofar as you can share equally with one another in the exercise of full democratic control of that community: you can play an equal part in controlling how the state imposes laws, punishes offenders, levies taxes, and thereby interferes in your lives.

These considerations answer the question as to whether the effective democratic control of government, were it achievable, would really mean that people did not suffer a lack of freedom in relation to the state. It would indeed mean this. But now we must turn to our second issue. Are there any institutions, in particular any feasible institutions, under which we might hope to establish or approach such democratic control: that is, hope to ensure that individuals have an equal share in the effective control of government?

Question 2: Is full democratic control capable of being achieved or approximated?

The notion of control—a notion that we have invoked in earlier discussions—involves two distinct elements: influence and direction. In order to appreciate what a democracy of popular control would involve, therefore, we have to understand what is required in order that there should be not only influence, but also direction. I look first at the distinction between influence and control; next, I consider how people could share equally in a system of influence over government; last, I explore the extent to which such a system of influence might impose a popular direction and make for an equally shared system of control.

Influence and Control

To influence a process is to make a difference in how the process evolves. To influence a process in a way that gives it direction is to make a designed difference, a difference that answers to some preconceived or preferred pattern. Control—that is, operative as distinct from just potential or reserve control—requires influence, but it also requires direction.[63]

Imagine that you pretend to be a police officer at a busy crossing, step out into the intersection, and give hand signals in the usual manner, acting as if you expected the cars to ignore the traffic lights. Some cars are likely to take their lead from your signals, despite the absence of a uniform, but others will undoubtedly follow the lights. You will certainly have an influence in such a case, making a difference to how the cars behave; you will probably create utter chaos. But will you have control? Not on the assumption that you wanted the cars to follow your signals. You will have made a difference to how the cars behave but not a difference that imposes any desired direction or pattern—not a difference that serves any identifiable end or goal.

What is required to give direction to the flow of cars and impose your operative control? Your influence must give rise to a recognizable pattern and that pattern must be one that you seek or welcome. There will be a range of ways in which you can vary your hand signals, and for each of those possible inputs, there must be a corresponding output in the movement of the cars: the traffic will take one or another path, depending on what signal you give. In the case where you stand at the intersection, this condition will not be fulfilled: there will be only a random correlation between the movement of your hands and the behavior of the cars. Were a police officer to be in your place, however, then things would be different. The officer's hand signals would reliably generate corresponding patterns in the movement of the traffic.

If the *demos* or people are to share equally in exercising *kratos* or power over government, and if the power they share is to mean that the coercive laws of government are not arbitrary and dominating, then what they exercise must constitute control. The people might have influence on government without this impressing any particular shape or pattern on the acts of government; the influence might be as wayward and random in its effects as the influence of the weather. That the people had such an influence would not lead us to think that the laws and decrees passed by government are passed on terms that they dictate.

This point of view is diametrically opposed to the model of democracy that is dominant in political science today. That model was proposed by Joseph Schumpeter in his classic book of 1942, *Capitalism, Socialism and Democracy*. Schumpeter (1984, 272) argues that democracy does not enable the people to "control their political leaders," holding—though not in so many words—that all it gives them is a wayward form of influence. He assumes, uncontroversially, that any plausible democratic system is going to involve open, periodic electoral competition, with different parties seeking to win office. Such a system is undoubtedly better than one of dynastic or chaotic succession, but Schumpeter is skeptical that it could give people control over government—that it would enable them to achieve "the realization of any definite end or ideal" (Schumpeter 1984, 253). The people do not form any agreed views, he says, that they might impose on leaders (253). And even if they did form such views, they would not be able to impose them; they would have little or no effect on the initiatives of the party boss and the party machine in "the competitive struggle for political power" (283). According to this deeply anti-republican model, democracy caters at most for the influence of the people—the influence of their aggregate pattern of voting—in selecting the party that will rule, not for anything resembling popular control.

Popular control, in republican theory, requires two conditions to be fulfilled. First, the people must have equal access to a system of popular influence over government: they must be entitled and enabled to share equally in operating that system, even if they cannot be forced to do so.[64] Second, that system of popular influence must impose on government a direction that all, given they accept their equality with others—given they accept that no one is special—have equal reason to welcome. I look now, but only very sketchily, at how such a system of equal influence and direction might be established (Pettit 2012c).

Making Popular Influence Attainable

Three problems and their resolution

A system of popular influence, equally accessible to all, could not involve a participatory assembly, even a virtual assembly, of all the citizens in a country; such a forum would preclude the discussion and deliberation required for coherent, collective decision-making (Pettit 2003). The only feasible way of organizing popular influence is via a familiar system: open, periodic, and competitive election to the legislature and perhaps also to other offices.[65] Such a pattern of election to public office is the only sure way of engaging and reinforcing the basic liberties of expression and association, thereby recruiting people to an enterprise of collective self-assertion and helping to underwrite the need for government to win popular acceptance.[66]

But, for a number of reasons, an electoral system is unlikely on its own to give people equal influence, even if almost all can and do vote, as under compulsory registration or voting, and even if electoral constituencies and rules ensure that each vote has the same value. It will fail to give them equal influence insofar as it fails to offer them the same chance of being on the winning side.[67] There are many problems that undermine the prospect of equal influence, but I shall mention three in particular: the sticky minority problem, the party interest problem, and the influential lobby problem.

The first problem is that some people may be locked into

a sticky minority—say, a religious minority with systematically divergent but neglected views—so that they lose out invariably in certain of the decisions taken by elected representatives. The second problem is that elected representatives, seeking to ensure their personal election or the election of their own party, will tend to exploit their powers in certain areas for electoral advantage; this abuse might occur in the drawing of electoral district boundaries, the setting of interest rates, or the reporting of economic and other data. And the third problem for establishing a regime of equally shared influence is that elected representatives are likely to be pressured and motivated to serve the interests of groups on which they depend for campaign finance or for favorable representation in the media; such lobbies are bound to be able, behind the backs of the public, to claim self-serving rewards for their efforts and thereby usurp the power of the state for their own advantage.

The solution to such problems requires dividing, constraining, regulating, and sometimes even sidestepping elected representatives. Take the sticky minority problem, for example, which can arise with any religious or ethnic or cultural minority, or with a minority distinguished by occupation, language, or sexual orientation. In order to resolve this barrier to equal influence, such groups must be enabled to find a public voice—most plausibly, via public interest organizations. And equally, they must be given a right of appeal to independent authorities for the assessment and, if necessary, rectification of their complaints. These authorities might include regular courts and special tribunals as well as ombudsmen, equality commissioners, and other watchdog agencies. They would make and enforce judgments on how far minority interests should be protected against majority rule if those in the minority are to count as equals—by received, popular criteria—in shaping the doings of government. They would identify issues on which sticky minorities are bound to be losers—say, issues about whether to privilege a majority religion or language or culture—and require such issues to be resolved on a nonmajoritarian basis or to be put off the agenda of government altogether.

Or again, take the party interest problem. Here the solution requires putting some public decisions at arm's length from elected deputies and/or establishing possibilities for the investigation and review of those elected to public life. It would argue for setting up an independent electoral commission with the authority to define electoral districts, a central bank with responsibility for setting interest rates, a bureau of statistics and an office of economic analysis that can offer authoritative snapshots of the society, and an auditor general who has the duty to inspect the government books. The solution to the party interest problem might even argue for assigning decisions or recommendations on sentencing policy to an independent body, given how the theater of electoral politics can mobilize a competition between politicians as to who is toughest on crime (Pettit 2002a). In each of these cases, moreover, it would support giving the principal officers involved a degree of independence from elected officials. They should be appointed according to set procedure and criteria and they should not be subject to dismissal at the pleasure of government.

Or consider finally the influential lobby problem, which jeopardizes the possibility of equal influence even more saliently than the others. In order to deal with this issue, there must be some means of regulating the financial support and the support of various media that politicians are bound to seek for themselves or their party. The measures that should be instituted to regulate financial support might include limits on individual contributions, limits or perhaps obstacles to the contributions that nonpolitical organizations can make, requirements of full disclosure on any finances supported, and maybe the provision of state support for electoral parties: this, as in many countries, can reduce the need and incentive to seek private backing. The measures that should be instituted to combat the power of those in the media might include a public media body independent of elected officials, which can play the role of ombudsman in receiving complaints, of watchdog in raising issues of concern, and of reviewer in investigating objections. They might also include setting up an independent public broadcaster such as the BBC or even, as may yet come to be necessary, an independent public newspaper, whether in print or digital format.

The three problems mentioned exemplify the difficulties in any system of popular influence that is built, as all plausible systems must be built, around electoral representation. The sorts of solutions at which I have gestured seem to be inescapable. They highlight the need to complement any electoral system with a constitutional or quasi-constitutional system that allows, on the one hand, for the appointment of regulatory and other authorities which can serve as independent checks on elected government, and on the other, for the mobilization of citizens in questioning and where necessary contesting government proposals and decisions. The organization of the citizenry for such purposes will require the establishment and recognition of a variety of public interest bodies that must develop enough expertise to cope with policy in a complex society. These will represent the views and interests of relatively vulnerable groups, not all of which are minorities: consumers as against producers, women as against men, immigrants as against the settled population, the unemployed as against the employed, the elderly as against those in the prime of life, and so on. Public interest bodies of the kind I have in mind are different from private lobbies insofar as they make their arguments in public and base their arguments on considerations that everyone can see as relevant: for example, considerations of equality and inclusion, accuracy in reporting, and fidelity to accepted precedent and tradition.

The proposed constitutional or quasi-constitutional system will have to serve familiar roles not mentioned here, laying down the rules governing the electoral process, the different branches of government, the different powers of those branches, and setting up an independent court system (Ely 1981). But whether in the form of a written document or an unwritten convention, it should also support the institutions required for ensuring a regime of equally shared influence, addressing the sticky minority, party interest, and influential lobby problems. Complementing the electoral system, it should seek to ensure by such measures that people enjoy equal access to the system of popular influence.

It is common in political theory to depict constitutional or quasi-constitutional provisions of these kinds as restrictions on democracy, fetters that stop the *demos* from exercising *kratos* in the undisciplined manner of a mob (Riker 1982). Constitutionalism of the sort proposed here, however, is not a force designed to thwart the power of the people but a means whereby that power can have effect. The proposal is for a democratically shaped constitutionalism, not for a constitutionally restricted democracy (Tully 2009). Constitutional provisions would constitute a thwarting force only if they did not have a role in channeling the influence of the people or if they were framed in a way that put them effectively beyond the reach of public discussion and reformation. But the provisions envisaged here are designed for the purpose of ensuring the equality of popular, democratic influence and are in no way insulated from popular interrogation and amendment.

Representation, electoral and non-electoral

The provisions supported are likely to provoke some opposition on the grounds that they would give excessive power to experts and professionals—legal–rational administrators, as they are often described. They would invest a range of unelected individuals and bodies with considerable authority, where the bearers of such power would not serve at the pleasure of government; while they would be open to dismissal according to set procedures, they could not be dismissed merely by government fiat. But what is to guarantee that such authorities would be representative of the people, acting only in the general interest and not for their own interests or those of some particular group? This worry, I suggest, can be addressed with the help of a richer understanding of the forms that representation may profitably take (Mansbrige 2009; Pettit 2009; 2010b).

Suppose I must nominate someone for a position on a committee. I might select someone whom I can require to consult with me and adopt my instructions on how to vote. Let us call such an appointee a responsive representative. But equally, I might select someone, even someone whom I cannot consult with or instruct, on the grounds that the person is likely to act as I would act, were I on the committee. Being someone whose decisions are indicative of what I would decide, we might describe this person as an indicative representative.

When we appoint ombudsmen, statisticians, and auditors to public office, the members of central banks and electoral commissions, and the judges who determine the interpretation and application of the law, we can appoint them under such tight constraints and with such precise briefs that they count as our indicative representatives. Unlike elected deputies, these authorities will be not be particularly responsive to specific popular demands; that is how we set things up. But if they operate in fidelity to their constraints and briefs, as popular scrutiny and vigilance can ensure that they do, then their decisions ought to conform to the protocols of their appointment and office. To the extent that they do conform to these expectations, they will act in a way that is indicative of how we the people—we who are ultimately responsible for the constraints and briefs that guide them—would want them to act. These officials will count as our indicative representatives. And like elective representatives, they will be exposed to a system of popular influence that we can all equally access.

As standing officials may count in this way as indicative representatives of the people, so the same is true of those who act on their own or via public interest groups to challenge or shape state policy. Such self-appointed agents operate under rules established within the system and are subject to formal and informal possibilities of counterchallenge. Whether or not we agree with what such agents seek in one or another area, we may regard them as playing a role that is indicative of the presumptive and frequently endorsed public concern for the interrogation of government initiatives and policies. We may cast them as indicative, if unofficial, representatives of the people.

While indicative representatives of an official or unofficial kind will help maintain a system of influence in which people equally share, we might also make use of indicatively representative bodies that can advise on particular matters. An excellent example of such a body is the British Columbia Citizens'

Assembly on Electoral Reform, though it is only one of many possible illustrations (Fishkin 1991; 1997; Sintomer 2007). This assembly was comprised of just over 150 citizens selected on a statistically representative basis. Thus, as the assembly voted on any issue, so we might expect that the population as a whole would have been disposed to vote. In other words, the assembly was designed to be indicatively representative of the population. The body was established by the provincial government of British Columbia, Canada, in 2004 and, meeting at regular intervals in the course of the year, it was asked to produce a recommendation on the voting system to be used in the province (Warren and Pearse 2008). The assembly opted for a change of system, but by government decree its recommendation had to win 60 percent support in a popular referendum if it was to be implemented. As things turned out, the change it proposed was supported by a little short of 59 percent of the electorate and did not therefore pass into law.

The Citizens' Assembly offers a model of how decisions on public policy might be informed by the findings of a temporarily convened body that is indicative of the population as a whole. It suggests that on many issues, in particular on issues where party interests may make it hard for politicians to give equal consideration to the interests of all, it would be good policy for a parliament or government to establish an ad hoc citizens' assembly. On such issues, a vocal minority with a vested interest in an outcome can make life very difficult for elected representatives to give equal concern to the interests of the often silent majority. Think, for example, of the issue raised by the introduction of a new road or rail route, or by the construction of a new public school or prison, or by the implementation of a new system of taxation. In any such case, a citizens' assembly could be given a role—either conclusive or advisory—in determining the resolution. It would guard against people's interests not weighing equally in the exercise of public influence.

The mixed constitution

The system of popular influence sketched here conforms in many respects to traditional republican ideals, wherein the social order established by government should be imposed by a mixed constitution, in the presence of an informed and powerful citizenry. Under a mixed constitution, as traditionally envisaged, things are organized according to standing rules that apply equally to all; those rules are adjusted on the basis of interaction among multiple, representative centers of power, not left in the control of any one individual or body; and the citizens who live under the rules have a crucial contestatory role in shaping them. The need for granting contestatory power to the people was particularly emphasized by Machiavelli (1965) in his *Discourses on Livy*.[68] He took the riotous Roman plebs to exemplify the contestatory disposition required for popular control of government. Other writers in the post-Machiavellian tradition maintained this emphasis, as when Adam Ferguson (1767, 167), an eighteenth-century Scot, traced the contestatory disposition to the "refractory and turbulent zeal" of any people fortunate enough to live under a government they could shape. He thought such zeal was required to ensure the eternal vigilance that, in words first attributed to his Irish contemporary, John Philpot Curran, was reckoned to be the price of liberty.

Although I have not presented the system of influence described here in such colorful terms, it fits well with this constitutional, contestatory template. The important contrast is with the idea, enshrined in Rousseau's communitarian ideal, that citizens should influence government by participating in every act of lawmaking or, as in later amendments, in the electoral process of choosing a plenipotentiary body of lawmakers. On our model it is important, on the one side, that no single, unconstrained body exercise lawmaking and other government functions, not even a body of the citizenry as a whole. And it is important, on the other, that citizens retain the right, outside the confines of any decision-making body, to contest and put a check on what government does. In the course of electoral participation, citizens will impose a collective check on government, of course, but they can play an equally important role in the opposition that they mobilize, whether in official forums, in the media, or on the streets. In the contemporary world, specialized public interest movements—movements in representation of consumers or women or prisoners, for instance—play a crucial role in streaming such complaints. The complexity of contemporary policy issues requires a division of civic labor in the scrutiny of different areas of policy-making, and nongovernmental organizations offer the only realistic hope of achieving an appropriate level of specialization.

Making Popular Direction Attainable

These brief comments should make clear why I think that there is a system of popular influence—a system inadequately realized in our actual arrangements—that people might equally access. But could such a system of popular influence impose a direction on government and, in particular, a direction that all, accepting that no one is special, have equal reason to welcome?

The possibility of democratic control
Looking at actual electoral systems, it may seem hard to avoid Schumpeter's conclusion that there is no prospect of establish-

ing a system that provides direction as well as influence. But Schumpeter only searches for a direction that people might be expected to impose in their active and short-term efforts in voting and campaigning. He overlooks the possibility that people might impose a direction over government in the longer term, relying on the following three factors: first, the existence of more established, albeit evolving attitudes in the electorate; second, the display of those attitudes in the things voters accept and reject out of hand both at election time and in ongoing contestation and discussion; and third, a recognition of those attitudes on the part of the authorities, elected and unelected, and a resulting disposition to adjust their preferred policies and processes in order to satisfy them.

I believe that a properly organized democracy can, over the long term, impose a direction on government that causes it to respond to such popular attitudes. In particular, I think that such a democracy can force a government to abide by community-wide standards in the processes of decision-making it follows and in the content of the decisions it makes.

Under a well-functioning system of popular influence of the kind we sketched, almost all public decisions are subjected to discussion, at one time or another, and exposed to public contestation and comment. While the different sides in such discussion and contestation will typically oppose one another, they will each mount a case for their viewpoint that is built on assumptions they think everyone can accept. To come to blows or simply walk away from one another would be to reject the most fundamental norm of democratic engagement—the norm of norms, we might call it—which is that no one is special and that the arguments made for any policy, or for any process of resolving policy differences, should be relevant from the standpoint of every adult, able-minded citizen.[69]

This constraint will be familiar from the school of thinkers who champion the cause of deliberative democracy, as it widely known (Cohen 1989; Dryzek 1990; Gutmann and Thompson 1996). It rules out the proposal of any policy or process on the simple, partial ground that it benefits a particular individual or group of individuals; there is no reason why others should regard that as a relevant consideration. The constraint would allow invoking impartial considerations that are clearly of relevance for all, such as considerations of equality or peace or prosperity or indeed conformity to established and expected practice. And it would allow invoking the needs or claims of a particular group in the case where there is a higher-level impartial consideration that argues for providing that group with special assistance or privilege. The argument might be that the subgroup suffers a disadvantage—say, a disability—against which everyone should have community insurance.[70] Or it might just be that the subgroup can be given a certain benefit without any loss to others.

Does the norm of norms in democratic engagement mean that certain groups, such as religious believers, are excluded from public discussion? Does it mean that they cannot speak from their most basic personal commitments in the forum of politics? Absolutely not. The norm allows those on all sides of society to voice their concerns and ideals, and to give them the most forceful and persuasive expression possible. What it requires is that in pressing for the arrangements under which they are to live with others, the partisans of different viewpoints have to recognize that they must find non-partisan considerations—considerations that all can see as relevant—to support their proposals. All members might agree, for example, on the importance of having arrangements that accommodate the deep commitments of those on rival, religious sides, recognizing at the same time that this must be balanced against the importance of not treating any members of the society as special. A model for such accommodation might be the arrangement under which conscientious objectors have been exempted from a period in military service, being required to spend a somewhat longer period in community service instead.

Suppose that a democracy operates over the long term in fidelity to the norm of norms, with the different parties seeking to base all proposals on considerations that everyone can recognize as relevant to the group project. The upshot ought to be the emergence of more particular norms or standards that establish relevant considerations in arguing about matters of public business. These considerations will have been tested and found acceptable across the community. Passing muster in public debate, the considerations can be invoked, without embarrassment, to support or oppose any decisions or any decision-making processes. They will constitute common norms or standards of political argument: trumps that anyone can play in support of the society's adopting a certain policy or procedure.

The rule of common standards

If this is right, then we should expect to see common standards of political argument acknowledged in any democratic society where public issues are resolved, at least in part, on the basis of open debate (Rawls 2001, 34–35). As a matter of fact, we do find this. Even in the United States, which is probably the most internally divided of advanced democracies, its people—or at least the 99 percent who are willing to live on equal terms with others—support a rich battery of shared standards, some of a basic egalitarian character, others more contingent in nature. Various egalitarian standards are spelled out in the country's constitution, especially in its amendments, such as those that require equal protection of the laws and the right of every citizen over eighteen to have and exercise the vote. But many equally important egalitarian standards have a less formal, if no less effective presence in political life. Examples might be the standard whereby separate no longer counts as equal, to invoke a slogan from the civil rights era, or the standard that supports the equality of women and men in the public square, in the workplace, and in the home.

Apart from egalitarian standards, there are a variety of other standards that govern public discourse in the US. And here there is also a divide between those that are reflected in provisions of the Constitution, as interpreted by Congress and the courts, and those that are not. Examples in the constitutional category are: that people should enjoy religious freedom, that religious schools should not be given state support, that speech should not be restricted just because it is false, that people have privacy rights no government should breach, and so on. Examples in the other, nonconstitutional category are: that victims of a natural catastrophe should receive public support, that government should monitor and preserve public health, that no child should be denied the chance of an education, that government statistics should be impartially collected, that public officials should declare and avoid conflicts of interest, and that in time of war conscientious objectors should not be equated with traitors or cowards.

In a well-functioning democracy, any policies proposed or any decision-making processes suggested will be discarded if on almost any plausible interpretation they flout local community-wide standards, as of course many will. The policies and processes that survive, then, will be supported by considerations that people all license as relevant and important. Answering to such considerations, they will impose a direction or pattern that is equally accepted by all, or at least by all who do not regard themselves as special. No policy that is objectionable by community-wide standards will pass into law. And of those policies in any domain that pass the bar of being unobjectionable—as many, of course, will—the one that is implemented will have to be selected under a process that those standards support.[71] This process might involve a parliamentary vote, referral to an independent body such as an electoral commission or central bank, recourse to an ad hoc commission of some kind, or even reliance on some form of lottery. The policies and processes implemented will not be uniquely determined by the community-wide standards, since much will depend on the contingent fact that this or that opinion commands a majority in a referendum, in the parliament, in a commission, or in the central bank, for example. But still, community-wide standards will substantively constrain the policies and processes that are chosen.

If policies and processes that breach community-wide standards are not filtered out effectively in a purportedly democratic society, that is a sign that the system of popular influence is not well designed or is not functioning effectively. The system may be excessively influenced by special lobbies or by elected representatives serving their own interests. Or it may be warped by restrictions on the rights of people to challenge their lawmakers, by unconstrained powers enjoyed by those authorities, or by the absence of an effective impartial media. Or the citizenry may underperform in keeping a vigilant eye on government; perhaps they may fail to display the refractory and turbulent zeal, in Adam Ferguson's words, that vigilance requires. The possibilities are legion and are amply illustrated in existing, all too imperfect regimes. Tolstoy wrote in the opening to *Anna Karenina* that "All happy families are alike; every unhappy family is unhappy in its own way." All democratic systems are alike, we might say; but every failing democracy fails in its own distinctive way.

If these observations are sound, then the main effect of a well-functioning democracy will be to make an infinite number of policies or processes unthinkable. The *demos* that keeps tabs and checks on government will mainly exercise *kratos*, not in causing this or that to be decided on, or to be decided on by this or that process, but in ensuring that a myriad of other policies and processes are never considered. They ride herd on the policies or decisions of those they elect, and on the decision-making processes whereby those policies are selected. They make sure that the authorities don't ever go off track and stand ready to blow the whistle—to make democratic trouble—if they do.[72] It may have been this pattern that traditional republicans had in mind when endorsing the idea that the price of liberty is eternal vigilance: that is, on this interpretation, eternal democratic vigilance.

The evidence of history
The long history of even quite imperfect democratic societies supports the view that a democratic people can exercise influence and impose this sort of long-term direction on government. In a series of classic studies, the historian Oliver MacDonagh (1958; 1961; 1977) has shown how Victorian England, under the impact of a growing democracy—under "the increasing sensitivity of politics to public pressures"—put in place a system of popular influence that inexorably generated a cascade of reforms, effecting a "transformation, scarcely glimpsed till it was well secured, of the operations and functions of government" (1958, 57–58). The pressures forced government, often against the personal inclinations of those in power, to regulate a great swathe of social behavior. This led to the creation of agencies that imposed strict inspection and control over such matters as the

employment of children, the treatment of women, the preparation of food and drugs, the organization of the civil service, and the conduct of affairs in mines and mills and factories.

The public pressures detailed by MacDonagh achieved this result in a manner that fits well with our account. In each area, the initial revelation of an evil led to popular outrage and popular outrage led to political response. That cycle of revelation, outrage, and response was played out again and again until public standards were satisfied and things ceased to be intolerable. "Once it was publicized sufficiently that, say, women on their hands and knees dragged trucks of coal through subterranean tunnels, or that emigrants had starved to death at sea or that children had been mutilated by unfenced machinery, these evils became 'intolerable'; and throughout and even before the Victorian years 'intolerability' was the master card" (1957, 58).

The legal and political commentators William Eskridge and John Ferejohn (2010) argue in a detailed examination of cases that popular pressure in the United States led in the same way to the implementation and entrenchment of certain norms: specifically, norms of equal citizenship, market openness, and personal security. Unconscious of the similarity of their argument to MacDonagh's narrative, they describe a process in which a social movement or other pressure creates a demand for state action; publicly supported legislation generates a statute embodying a new norm; the statute is administered and expanded with feedback and pushback from various sectors of the community; the norm is revisited and reaffirmed by the legislature in face of opposition; and this is followed by further administrative elaboration, further feedback and pushback, and further legislative revision (Eskridge and Ferejohn 2010, 19–20). Like MacDonagh, they illustrate the slow emergence and impact of popular norms that I see as evidence of the effect that democracy can have in imposing a direction on government.

The mention of Victorian England or contemporary America ought not to suggest that either represents even a close approximation of what would count, by republican lights, as a well-functioning democracy. Victorian England did not give everyone the vote and ensured a privileged place for those in the upper classes. And America has long been blighted by what John Rawls (1999) described as "the curse of money," providing the wealthy and powerful with an extraordinary degree of influence and control over those whom the people elect. But even such shortfalls from the republican ideal of democracy were not enough in either case to block the emergence and impact of certain community-wide standards of policy-making.

Slow and fast democracy
On the picture emerging from these considerations, democracy can give people an equally shared form of directed influence or control over government, and can do so in some measure even when it falls short of relevant ideals. But democracy achieves this effect over the long haul, not in a particular round of election or challenge. When asking about whether people exercise a directed as distinct from a wayward influence over government, it is tempting to look for evidence in specific actions, particularly in the actions whereby they elect a party to government or put it out of office. Schumpeter takes this approach, and it leads inevitably to skepticism about the existence of any form of popular control over government, let alone a form that is equally shared among people. But once we pull back from the detail of particular elections and challenges and look at democratic government over the *longue durée*, we see a rather more heartening pattern. However imperfect this pattern may be, it offers

evidence of how deeply its people can shape a government, if only they are given the full instruments of influence that we have charted here.

It is important to register the possibility that a people, organized so as to have equal access to influence, can impose such a direction on government. This possibility keeps alive the ideal of a democracy rooted in popular control rather than the lesser ideal of a democracy of popular influence. In requiring a system in which people have equal access to a directive form of influence, the ideal of popular control supports institutional measures that are much more demanding than those the rival ideal would support.

The Tough Luck Test

We saw earlier that, if they shared equally in effective control of government, people would escape state domination and preserve their freedom on this front. And we have just now identified the sorts of institutions that would enable people to impose a welcome pattern on government decisions and bring it under a degree of equally shared control. But would the control mediated by such institutions be effective enough—would the pattern be sufficiently constraining—to ensure that government interference was not dominating: that is, did not represent the presence of an alien will and power in people's lives?

The tough luck test, mentioned in the prologue, serves the same role in determining the adequacy of guards against public domination that the eyeball test serves in determining the adequacy of guards against private domination. The idea behind the test is that the control achieved under the democratic institutions envisaged will be enough to guard against government domination if it enables people to think that when public structures and policies and decisions frustrate their personal preferences, that is just tough luck. By local standards of when loopholes are tolerable and trust appropriate, there is no reason for people to take such unwelcome constraints as the work of a malign will that imposes itself on them or their kind—or, indeed, on ordinary citizens as a whole.

Suppose that the policies implemented under a well-functioning system are to a particular subgroup's disadvantage. If the system is operating properly, then members of that subgroup will be able to test the decision-making at one or another contestatory site: via judicial challenge, for example, complaint to an ombudsman, or public protest. And they should be assured thereby—by local standards of assurance—that the process employed and the policy implemented in the decision were both compatible with accepted norms: that is, compatible with the community-wide standards that all accept. Thus they ought to be able to regard the upshot as a matter of bad fortune.

If the final decision was determinately selected, then it was required under relevant norms. And if it was not determinately selected—if it was just one of many possible, norm-compatible results—then it was the product of norm-compatible process: it was chosen by parliament or by an independent authority, in a referendum or under the instructions of a court. Either way, so they can think, it was just tough luck. It was tough luck that the site chosen for the prison was in their neighborhood, for example; or that the tax regime selected worked against their particular interests; or that the immigration laws passed made it difficult for them to sponsor the immigration of other members of their family.[73]

The tough luck test is quite demanding, since it will support approval for a democratic regime only if that regime really gives people equally accessible influence and imposes an equally acceptable direction. If the electoral system is skewed against the interest of a particular group, then members of that group will not be able to think that some unwelcome decision was just tough luck; it will be more plausible to think that government policy reflects the malign will of a body that is not constrained to consider their interests. Equally, if the electoral system allows decisions to be made away from the possibility of contestation, or without suitable outside constraints, then the members of a group that suffers from such decisions have no reason to think that it was just tough luck that they and not others were disadvantaged. It will be much more plausible to think that they are discriminated against by an ill-willed agency. And the same will hold, of course, if the courts or commissions or other decision-making bodies are selected on a discriminatory basis or if they are allowed to make their decisions in an equally unconstrained or incontestable manner. A society will pass the tough luck test only if people truly enjoy an equally accessible form of influence that channels government—that is, the legislature, the executive, the judiciary, and other decision-making bodies—in an equally acceptable direction.

In discussing freedom in the first part of the book, I quoted Kant (2005, 11) to the effect that while being "dependent on many external things" is hard, "the subjection of one human being under the will of another" is much harder still. What democracy would ideally ensure for the subjects of a government is that when things go against them, this is not the sign of subjection to a malign will. It is a product of tough luck. The disadvantages imposed may certainly be regrettable, but they need not be cause for resentment. Under the ideal envisaged here, they may be as blindly and blamelessly imposed as a misfortune wrought by the natural world.

THE BOTTOM LINE

As depicted in this chapter, republican democracy is an essentially emergent and essentially evolving institution. It is emergent in the sense that the control it gives the people emerges from the interaction of many different bodies operating at many different points and in many different ways; it is built on the basis of a mixed constitution (Vermeule 2011). And it is evolving in the sense that that popular control may only appear over the longer run, and not in every decision-making instance; it is an essentially slow, and ideally developing process.

How does this republican image of an emergent, evolving democracy compare with competitors in policy-making terms? First, it gives much greater importance to democracy than do many other theories. And, second, it is much more demanding about the institutions that a democracy ought to put in place.

The importance that democracy receives in republican theory shows up primarily in the fact that the theory requires democracy to serve a normatively central role—that of protecting the citizens of a state against public domination by the government. Because it meets that requirement, the democratic state can make a morally powerful demand on its citizens to oppose its decisions only within the system, and not without. Not dominating citizens in the treatment it affords them, it can make a uniquely compelling claim to be a legitimate, coercive arbiter on issues where citizens are divided (Pettit 2012c, Richardson 2002).

The reason why a state that meets the republican specification is legitimate in this sense is that it does not take from the freedom of citizens; it operates on terms that they impose. But the connection that republican theory makes between democracy and freedom is enough in itself to emphasize the importance that it gives democracy. It restores life to the long-standing association in popular thought between the two values and marks a contrast in this respect with approaches that cast freedom as noninterference.

On the view that freedom means just noninterference, democracy does not serve the cause of freedom in any distinctive way, as thinkers from William Paley to Isaiah Berlin have recognized. If freedom consists in noninterference, then coercive government, democratic and nondemocratic alike, necessarily takes away from people's freedom. Hence the only question will be whether democracy tends to do better in reducing overall interference than rival systems: whether it achieves a better balance between the interference it prevents and the interference it perpetrates. Thus Paley (2002, 314) wrote in 1785 that "an absolute form of government" may be "no less free than the purest democracy." And Berlin (1969, 130) sounds the same theme, nearly two hundred years later, when he opines that "there is no necessary connection between individual liberty and democratic rule."[74]

There may be reasons why democracy is important, of course, apart from the role it plays in legitimating government and apart from its connection with the freedom of people under government. Indeed, there are a number of theories that argue for its importance on other grounds: for example, that it helps to maintain political equality, or to make government more reliable in its judgments, or to give deliberation a proper role in public affairs, or just to guard against dynastic rule.[75] But no competing theory gives it the same incontrovertible importance as the republican approach sketched here. And most fail to give it any distinctive job at all. They take democracy as an institutional given, associating it with the requirement of periodic, competitive election, and then look to see what particular merits it may have.

Not only does the republican approach give enormous importance to democracy, however; it also argues for quite demanding, though plausible constraints on democratic procedure. Republican theory rejects the Romantic image of democracy, probably of Rousseauvian origins, in which the people govern themselves in assembly, on the grounds that it is manifestly unworkable. Apart from problems of size, an assembly arrangement would jeopardize the proper consideration and reconsideration of policy proposals: it would be just too large or too cumbersome to make this possible (Pettit 2012d). But however un-Romantic in that respect, the theory envisages a role for initiatives in public consultation of the kind illustrated in the British Columbia Citizens' Assembly. And most important of all, it imposes stringent egalitarian demands on how people can exercise influence on government. To the extent to which such equality of influence fails, there will be less hope of community-wide standards emerging and constraining government.

Thus the theory requires, for a start, that a democratic regime should be deeply inclusive: ideally, I would say, inclusive to the point of requiring electoral registration for all and even making voting compulsory (Hill 2000). At the same time, it should make space for popular contestation—and for measures that would force government to take heed of such contestation—by establishing ombudsman and similar offices for hearing complaints, and by appointing regulatory agents such as auditors and comptrollers to monitor government on the public's behalf. Again, it would make government less likely to trigger contestation, and more likely to be responsive to contestation, by assigning troublesome functions to unelected authorities who would exercise precise briefs under rigorous constraints. And it would search for institutional devices to shut down the myriad, financially lubricated channels whereby special interests seek a warping influence on government: an influence that is not sought in public space or not urged on public grounds.

While it envisages a constitutional system for establishing checks on those channels, and for putting the other required measures in place, the theory argues for exposing the constitution itself to public interrogation and to the permanent possibility of reform. Most significantly, it envisages and designs the system as a means of furthering democracy—a means of promoting the equality and effectiveness of public control—and not as a brake on what democracy can achieve. Thus, where it argues for the appointment of certain unelected authorities, it would expose both those authorities and their elected counterparts to the permanent possibility of being called to account. Almost all such officials and bodies can be called to account by other authorities within the system, but the job of calling them to account falls ultimately to the citizenry both at times of election and in specific, targeted criticism and protest.

The commitment to contestation on the part of the citizenry does not argue for heroic individual attempts to exercise vigilance over all aspects of government. In a complex contemporary society, the only hope of a systematic, encompassing interrogation of government lies with public interest movements and bodies. Operating in public space, and guided by publicly accepted standards, such nongovernmental organizations can specialize in different domains and develop the expertise required for keeping tabs on the performance of government as a whole. One organization will specialize in consumer affairs, another in health policy, another in women's rights or the rights of a minority, another in prison conditions, and yet another in the plight of the homeless. The best hope for a flourishing democracy lies with the prospect of a people who are active and engaged enough to give life to such movements and of authorities who are willing—willing and electorally forced—to give recognition and attention to these, their harshest critics.

No theory would count as a theory of democracy unless it kept faith at a general level with the sorts of institutions that we find in most democracies today. Thus it should be no surprise that the notes struck in the theory outlined here resonate in each case with more or less familiar democratic arrangements. But still, the theory is highly demanding since it holds out a goal for democracy that few if any existing arrangements come even close to matching.

Looking at our oldest continuing democracy, that of the United States, the institutional template sketched reveals shortfalls and offenses of egregious proportions. These include systematically supported restrictions on the opportunity to vote; the gerrymandering of electoral districts for party purposes; the private financing of electoral campaigns and the presumptive paybacks it secures; the power given to corporations, and effectively their CEOs, to join in this scramble for favor; the massively funded lobbying exercised by private interests; the dominance of openly partisan, unreliable media organizations; the forced deference to party extremes that the primary system encourages; the near impossibility of significant amendments to the Constitution; and the power of a Supreme Court whose members are appointed for life under an effectively politicized process that rewards party profile. This motley list reminds us of the importance of developing and maintaining a critical theory of the goal of democracy and of the institutions that are essential for achieving that goal; otherwise, we are likely to lose a sense of where we should be aiming. I believe that the republican theory sketched in this chapter fits that bill.

Chapter 6

FREEDOM AND SOVEREIGNTY

We saw in the first part of this book that in order for people to enjoy something approaching the traditional republican ideal of freedom as non-domination, their freedom of choice would have to be resourced and protected to a suitable depth, over a suitable breadth or range of choice. People would be free in a choice to the extent that they had the ability to choose between the options, regardless of their preference and regardless also of the preference of other agents as to what they should do. And they would count as free persons or citizens to the extent that they enjoyed such freedom of choice on the basis of public resourcing and protection across the range of the basic liberties, as these are identified in their own society.

In chapters 4 and 5 we looked at what such freedom of the person requires in institutional terms, focusing on a single society. We argued that in order to enjoy freedom in relation to one another, people would have to be equally resourced and protected against private domination by the state. In order to preserve and enjoy freedom in relation to the public power of the state, they would have to share equally in controlling the use of that power, whether directly or indirectly, via election or contestation or regulation. This implied that people would have to enjoy an intuitive ideal of justice in their private lives and an intuitive ideal of democracy in their public. The two sets of requirements gave us an appealing, republican conception of justice on the one hand and democracy on the other.

These twin republican ideals require, to coin a slogan, that people should live under an undominating defender against domination. But, looking beyond the confines of a single society, there is a further ideal that freedom as non-domination requires us to establish as well. The state that defends people's freedom must not only be undominating or democratic, considered from an internal viewpoint. It must also be undominated by any other state or by any international or multinational body. If such a state were dominated by an outside agency, then its citizens would also be dominated by that agency, since any restrictions at the level of the state would inevitably involve restrictions on their democratic lives. And so we see that the ideal of the free person or citizen requires that the state that protects people against private domination ought to be, not only internally undominating, but externally undominated as well.

FROM STATES TO PEOPLES

Our aim in this chapter is to explore the international form assumed by the ideal of republican liberty—the ideal of external non-domination—and these introductory remarks may suggest that we ought to think of this as an ideal of externally undominated states. But that suggestion, as we must now see, can't be quite right.

It may be appealing to hold that democratic states ought not to be externally dominated, where democratic governments are composed of responsive and indicative representatives. In these democratic states, some authorities are subject to a high degree of causal control by their citizenry, thereby counting as responsive representatives. Other authorities are subject to such constraints of appointment and review that they may be expected to act in accord with community views, thereby counting as indicative representatives. And both sorts of authorities, who may overlap in some measure, are required to coordinate their activities so that, assuming a suitable system of coordination, the government or state that they constitute can claim to act and speak in its people's name: it can be cast as representative of its people.[76] It is because democratic states are presumptively representative of their peoples in this manner that the ideal of external non-domination of a democratic state is appealing. It amounts to the ideal of external non-domination of the people of that state, where the people can be considered either as a collection of individuals or as a collective agent that exists insofar as there is an organ—the state—that acts and speaks in its name (List and Pettit 2011).

But while it is certainly appealing to cast the external non-domination of democratic and representative states as an ideal, it may not be appealing in the same measure to look for the external non-domination of undemocratic or unrepresentative states. Take a state that is so ineffective—so divided within itself or so bereft of resources—that it does not have the capacity to represent its people; it is unable to discharge some of the most basic functions of a state, whether in the area of infrastructure, insurance, or insulation. Or take the state that is not so much ineffective as oppressive: it has the capacity to discharge the basic functions of the state but rather than doing so—or rather than doing so, at least, for all of its citizens—it actively oppresses a smaller or larger proportion of its population. To hail the external non-domination of an ineffective or oppressive state as an ideal would be madness; it could amount to licensing whole-sale mayhem or murder.

What form should the ideal of republican liberty assume in the international arena, if it is not to be an ideal of external non-domination for states? The most plausible answer, in light of what we have just said, is: the external non-domination of peoples. For each state, representative or unrepresentative, there is a people: a population of individuals at one level and at another, at least potentially, a collective people that can organize itself via a representative state. Whether or not a people enjoys internal non-domination—whether or not it enjoys democracy—it must still count as an evil, in the republican ledger, that that people should be dominated by an external body, be this a state, a multinational corporation, or an international agency. And so the ideal of republican liberty, transported to the international arena, can be seen as an ideal of externally undominated peoples; in that respect, it is akin to the ideal pursued by John Rawls (1999) under the title *The Law of Peoples*.

The republican ideal is an ideal for all the peoples of the earth, whether or not they are democratically organized. It calls for a global framework in which each people is entrenched against domination from other states and from the various non-state actors—agencies, churches, corporations—that have international dimensions. This ideal offers a plausible interpretation of what international justice requires in current arrangements: I ignore issues of historical justice. I describe it as an ideal of globalized sovereignty: that is, sovereignty extended to every people on earth.[77]

THE IDEAL OF GLOBALIZED SOVEREIGNTY

The early modern absolutists Jean Bodin and Thomas Hobbes introduced the notion of sovereignty, as we saw, in criticizing the republican idea that a state could be organized under a mixed constitution, which divides out power among different bodies. They argued that a single individual or body within the state has to enjoy absolute power if the state is to perform as a reliable, coherent agent. The ideal of sovereignty invoked here does not bear on the internal organization of the state, however; in the previous chapter, indeed, we explicitly defended a mixed, republican constitution. The ideal of globalized sovereignty belongs wholly to the international sphere. It requires that however their states are organized internally, the peoples of the world should not be dominated by foreign states or by other internationally operative agencies or bodies.

The ideal of globalized sovereignty does not downgrade the importance of individuals, prioritizing the needs of the societies or states that they constitute. To the extent that a people, taken as a whole, is subject to the control of an external agency, that agency will dominate the individuals who compose the people. And a concern for the status of those individuals—a concern for their escaping domination—is enough on its own to give support to the ideal of globalized sovereignty. Let a people as a whole be dominated—that is, the people considered as at least a potential collective agent—and the individual members of that people will be dominated; any restrictions will reduce their individual democratic effectiveness. And, plausibly, it is this impact on individuals that argues for the importance of international sovereignty among the peoples of the world.[78]

As the republican ideal of democracy gives us an ideal of

political as distinct from social justice, so the ideal of sovereignty gives us an ideal of international justice. It suggests the high ideal of a just world in which each people can stand on its own feet, enjoying the objective and subjective status of a free people in its international relations. As the free citizens of a just and democratic state will be each entrenched on a public basis in the enjoyment of certain basic liberties, so in this ideal the free peoples of the world would be each entrenched on a public, international basis in the enjoyment of a corresponding set of internationally recognized sovereign liberties.

We saw in earlier chapters that the republican ideals of justice and democracy far outrun anything that has been achieved in national politics anywhere, although each ideal remains within reach. The same is true, and in trumps, of the republican ideal of a sovereignty of peoples. Although the ideal is far from utopian, the international order fails to realize it in two conspicuous ways. First of all, many peoples do not have a democratic state—or any plausibly representative state—to speak for them and to claim sovereignty in their name; they are ruled by oppressive or ineffective governments. Second, even democratic, representative states have failed to establish an order in their mutual relationships that reliably provides each with a proper independence from the will and power of other states or of non-state actors.

This observation suggests that we should break our discussion of the republican ideal of a sovereignty of peoples into two parts. In the first, I will concentrate on a world of suitably representative states, looking at the ways each such state, and each such people, might come to have a sovereign status in relation to other states and to non-state actors. In the second part of the discussion, I will look at the implications of that ideal for our actual world, where some states fail to be representative of their peoples, either through being ineffective or through being oppressive.[79]

This division of labor presupposes the possibility of distinguishing more or less cleanly between representative and non-representative states: between states that can claim to act and speak for their peoples and states that are too impoverished or oppressive to do so credibly. Up to this point, I have associated representative states with fully democratic states. But it may be useful to loosen that association and recognize that effective, generally non-oppressive states can claim to have a certain representative status, despite falling well short of democracy. None of the authorities that combine to operate such states may be elected in a meaningful way, yet the effective, non-oppressive manner in which they operate may show that they can reasonably claim to be indicative representatives of their subjects. And if they are indicative representatives of this kind, then there is a recognizable sense in which the state they operate can claim to act and speak for its people.[80]

My own view is that nothing less than full democracy can be normatively satisfactory, grounding the obligation of citizens to oppose the laws, if they oppose them, only within the system (Pettit 2014b). But still, it is reasonable to extend the category of representative states beyond the category of democratic states. A full democracy would have the effect of making a state robustly representative: the government would be under such control that even if it wished, it could hardly cease to be guided by its people and to count as their representative. But short of a state's being robustly representative in that sense, it may fall in line with the standards of the community to a sufficient degree and with sufficient resilience to claim representative status. The party that is in power may not be democratically answerable to the people, for example, but its hold on power may depend on promoting the economic and social welfare of its citizens and to that extent it may be fairly effectively constrained by consideration of their interests.

In what follows, I shall assume that representative states—in effect, states that are both effective and non-oppressive—need not be democratically organized. This is convenient as well as reasonable, since it would be unrealistic to reduce the states that are given the principal role in our international theory to ones that are fully democratic, or even democratic in a substantial measure. I leave open the concrete question as to which actual states fall on which side of this divide between the representative and the nonrepresentative. Indeed, I can even leave open the more abstract issue as to how exactly to articulate the distinction. However exactly the distinction is articulated, it will allow the argument that follows to go through.

BUT SHOULD THERE BE STATES?

We are now in a position to engage the first stage of our investigation, exploring what the ideal of globalized sovereignty would mean in a world of representative states. Before we begin, however, I should comment on the assumption that we can take the existence of states for granted in addressing international justice. Why not consider the possibility of a stateless world, or a world with one world state? We saw earlier that a combination of historical, political, and functional necessities has given us a world of many states, but the question now is whether a concern with freedom gives us grounds for preferring a different sort of world.

I ignore the possibility of a stateless world on the grounds, mentioned in the previous chapter, that there is no real possibility of establishing social justice without relying on the coercive power with which the state, as a functional necessity, imposes laws. If the state is necessary, however, why not have a single state rather than a profusion of states?

In the abstract, a world state might work very well. But in a world where cultures vary enormously, agreed policy-making norms would be unlikely to crystallize in the way they can in a more closely connected society. And in a world where trust is often in short supply across cultural divides, there would be less likelihood of establishing those important unelected authorities—judges, ombudsmen, election commissioners, central bankers, and the like—who could credibly claim to make decisions in line with shared standards. Think of the dissatisfaction and distrust of European Union officials that began to appear as soon as the Eurozone crisis resurrected nationalistic feelings and antipathies. And now imagine how much worse this would be if there were a world state that had to cope with a similar crisis. Thus the cause of democracy, articulated in terms of freedom, argues for a world of many states. And even if that is not persuasive, mere realism would argue for focusing our prescriptions on a world in which there are many distinct states; we are unlikely to see another sort of world in the feasible or foreseeable future.[81]

Suppose, then, that there is no reason, or at least no freedom-based reason, to prefer a stateless or one-state world to the actual world of many states. The ideal of freedom as non-domination entails in the context of this assumption that each state has special obligations toward its own citizens: it should seek to introduce laws that guard against private domination and to introduce them on a basis that guards against public domination. Only their own state can serve this function for citizens. And so each state has obligations to its own citizens of a kind that it does not have toward the citizens of any other state (Nagel 2005). If the citizens of other regimes are to fare well in relevant dimensions, that depends on the performance of their own state in exercising its special obligations toward them.

This observation argues against the idea of cosmopolitan justice, currently fashionable in some circles, according to which there is no difference between the obligations that a state has toward its own citizens and those that it has toward human beings in general, in particular the citizens of other states (Beitz 1979; Pogge 1993; Caney 2005).[82] But while a state may have special obligations toward its own citizens, under an approach that prioritizes freedom as non-domination, it does not follow that it owes nothing to the citizens of other states. On the contrary, as we shall see, the value of freedom means that if individuals in other states do not fare well, say because their state is impoverished or oppressive, then other states will have certain obligations of assistance toward them.

We can now return to the main theme. We must first ask about the significance of the ideal of globalized sovereignty for a world of representative states. And then we must explore the duties of states toward peoples who do not have states to represent them: peoples who live under ineffective or oppressive regimes. Taking up the first task, I look first at how deep the sovereign freedom of representative states ought to be and then at the breadth of choices over which representative states ought to be able to exercise that freedom. The task is parallel to the task taken up in the first part of the book, when we looked at the depth of freedom as non-domination in individual choice and then at the breadth of choices in which such freedom should be available.

THE DEPTH OF THE SOVEREIGNTY IDEAL

In 1648, most of the states in the religious wars that had devastated Europe for thirty years agreed to a set of treaties signed in two towns, Münster and Osnabrück, both situated in Westphalia, now a part of the German republic. The Westphalian treaties established a settlement in the religious divisions that had pitted prince against prince, country against country. The slogan that came to exemplify the resolution achieved was *cujus regio, ejus religio*: whoever rules a region dictates the religion of that region. The resolution meant, on the positive side, that the ruler of each country was to be the ultimate authority in all matters within its boundaries, even in the matter of the religion of its subjects. On the negative side, it meant that no one was entitled to intervene in any other country; rulers should keep their noses out of one another's business.

The Westphalian orthodoxy, which ruled international affairs until the last century, takes the sovereignty of a country to consist in nonintervention, as nonrepublican theories take the freedom of an individual to consist in noninterference. Unsurprisingly, then, the republican ideal breaks with this pattern, casting sovereignty on the model of the republican ideal of freedom. It holds that whatever choices are to lie within the power of a people—we will discuss the desirable range or breadth of choice in a moment—they ought to be able to exercise those choices without domination from outside. It is not enough that the state that represents them should manage to escape intervention. It is essential that it be able to escape intervention regardless of the will of other states and other international agencies. It ought not to have to depend on the goodwill of any other body for enjoying the absence of intervention.

We saw that one agent interferes in the choices of another by removing, replacing, or misrepresenting available options. One state is unlikely to be able to intervene in the choices of another on the basis of misrepresenting options—except in the case of bluffing threats that are taken seriously by the threatened—but a state can certainly intervene in either of the two other ways. It can make options more costly by imposing or threatening to impose penalties of one or another kind: military penalties or, in an interdependent world like ours, penalties of an economic, financial, cultural, or diplomatic kind. And it can make certain options more or less impossible by imposing barriers—to trade or otherwise—or by fixing relevant agendas. Insofar as one state has a power of intervening in any of these ways in the affairs of another—in particular, a power against which the other state cannot protect itself defensively or by retaliation—it will dominate that other state. And any such form of domination will offend against the republican ideal of sovereignty.

This means that the republican ideal of sovereignty is deeper than the Westphalian ideal, as the republican ideal of individual freedom is deeper than the classical liberal ideal. You can be personally dominated by being subject to my power of interference and dependent on my goodwill, even if I do not interfere in your life. Similarly, a state can be dominated by the presence of another state that can intervene at will in its internal affairs, whether by military, economic, or other means. And it can be dominated in this way even if the other state never actually intervenes. The ideal of freedom requires us to guard against domination without interference as well as domination with interference. And the ideal of sovereignty requires us to guard against domination without intervention as well as domination with intervention.

As a people or state can be dominated by other states, of

course, so it can be dominated by non-state actors—international agencies, multinational corporations, world churches, and the like—that have a power of intervening in some area of policy, even a power that is not actually exercised. The Roman Catholic Church in medieval and early modern Europe exercised a certain domination over secular states, having powers like those of excommunication or interdiction. And multinational corporations often dominate contemporary states, having a power over government that derives from being able to move their operations elsewhere and to beggar the economy. In this discussion, I will concentrate on the state–state case, though most of the points to be made apply in other relations too.

THE BREADTH OF THE SOVEREIGNTY IDEAL

Thus, if a representative state and its people are to enjoy sovereignty in relation to other states—and in relation to other international bodies—they must be entrenched in quite a deep manner against any domination. The entrenchment will require them to be protected under international practice against potentially dominating agencies, though not in the normal run to be resourced on this front; representative states will generally have all the resources needed. But, as with individuals, this entrenchment cannot extend across the range of all the possible choices the state might make. So what are the choices in which a representative state ought to be protected, if not resourced? What are the choices that it should be able to make, regardless of its own preferences among the options and regardless also of the preferences of other states and bodies in regard to how it chooses? What are the sovereign liberties, as we may call them, that should be accorded to representative states under international arrangements?

It may seem plausible to hold that the sovereign liberties accorded to any representative state, and so to any people, should comprise all and only the co-enjoyable choices possible in the international arena, as the basic liberties accorded to an individual should encompass all and only the co-enjoyable choices available within a domestic society. But this is not quite right, since there is a special constraint on the liberties that any state should be accorded. It should not have any freedom of choice that would undermine the possibility of its citizens enjoying non-domination in the sphere of the basic liberties. Thus, under the ideal of globalized sovereignty—by contrast with the Westphalian ideal—no state should be allowed a discretion that would reduce the scope of people's basic liberties, as in being able to determine their religion.

Assuming that this internal constraint on the range of a state's choices is satisfied, however, we can return to the formula given and say that each representative state and people should enjoy all and only those sovereign liberties that are consistent with the enjoyment of similar liberties on the part of other representative states and peoples. These liberties should involve choices that can be established under international arrangements in which all states have equal standing. Each state should be capable of exercising any such liberty at the same time that other states exercise it, and the simultaneous exercise of those liberties should be satisfying, so far as possible, from the point of view of all.

So what liberties ought to be established among states? There will be some clear candidates for implementation, such as liberties of speech, expression, and association. But many other cases will be more problematic, as with the liberty of exploring national resources, exploiting common resources, organizing mutual trading privileges, and the like. The cowboy and the farmer can be friends, we argued, only under rules that establish co-exercisable, co-satisfying choices for them, and the same, arguably, is true here. With suitable rules in place, states can each enjoy the freedom to explore the resources on their own territory and to trade with one another in the products of such exploration. Again, with suitable rules in place, they can each exploit common resources—say, the fish in international waters—in a sustainable, shared manner. And with suitable rules in place, they can actively work at providing in the international world for counterparts to the infrastructure, insurance, and insulation that the domestic state provides for its citizens. They can cooperate in establishing a system of liberties that allows for the creation of global public goods in domains like international trade, public health, and scientific research, and that guards against global public bads like atmospheric pollution or climate change.

The need for international cooperation in establishing a pattern of reform and adjustment in the face of climate change is probably the most powerful challenge facing the international community today (Broome 2012). Another challenge involves the increasing power of multinational corporations and banks to warp government policies by playing countries against one another in a search for ever lower levels of taxation and ever more lenient standards of environmental and financial regulation. The most frequent threat in each country is to move offshore, beggaring the local economy or embarrassing local officials, and it can only be countered by universal standards set through international cooperation.

The rules establishing what each country may and may not be able to do in such respects need to be negotiated in international forums. The difficulties of successful negotiation in such matters are enormous, but more has been achieved on this front since World War II than in all of previous history. And however difficult it may be to achieve results in this area, a system of agreed and accepted rules is an absolute prerequisite for a regime of globalized sovereignty. I argued earlier that basic liberties are not a natural kind, and require identification under local rules and conventions. What holds for basic liberties holds on the same grounds, and much more saliently, for sovereign liberties. States can hope to enjoy freedom and sovereignty in relation to other states and other international bodies only under an internationally agreed, and internationally institutionalized, set of rules and conventions.

ENTRENCHING THE SOVEREIGNTY IDEAL

Let us assume that a system of sovereign liberties can be articulated on the basis of negotiation between different states in the international world. Those liberties will be worth little unless there is reason to assume that representative states can also be expected to uphold them, providing one another with all the resourcing and protection that the enjoyment of non-domination requires. So what are the prospects for institutionally entrenching any liberties that might be identified as suitable? What are the prospects, in effect, for implementing the sovereignty ideal?

Assuming that proposed liberties are identified in negotiation, or gain recognition in customary international law, the fact that certain states recognize and honor those liberties will presumably attract the approval of the states and peoples that benefit from their behavior, as well as in the world at large. Like individuals, states may be expected to seek such approval and to shrink from disapproval, if only because esteemed states will tend to enjoy more opportunities for international influence than states that are less esteemed. And so we can expect them, on pain of losing approval or earning disapproval, to be pressured and policed into honoring one another's sovereign liberties.[83] Thus, the negotiated articulation of a system of sovereign liberties will naturally be supported by the emergence of social norms, to invoke a concept introduced earlier, requiring respect for the recognized liberties. These norms can be greatly strengthened, of course, if they are spelled out and given support in international forums or in forums convened for the purpose of determining binding norms (Goodin and Ratner 2011).

But is the esteem-based pressure of global norms the only force that we can expect to channel states toward the recognition of one another's sovereign liberties? No, it is not. Other things being equal, the self-interest of every state will argue, not just for condemning any offenses against its own liberties, but also for condemning any offenses against the liberties of other countries as well. For it is only if states are willing to uphold the system of sovereign liberties in a general manner that they can expect to be able to rely on it as a means for protecting themselves. There may be a temptation for some states to free-ride, of course, seeking to benefit from the sovereign liberties available to all while placing the burden of enforcement on others. But the community of states is small enough, and the chance of detection high enough, for this not to be a chronic problem.

The expectation that representative states might cooperate with one another in entrenching a system of sovereign liberties is not fanciful. Even within the existing global framework, however inadequate, there are a number of international agencies, set up on the basis of multilateral treaties, that serve a centralized, ordering role in the relations between states. They establish, monitor, and enforce the impartial rules that determine, in our sense, the shape of sovereign liberties (Keohane 1984). These bodies include the United Nations, of course, insofar as it plays the role of maintaining peace both between hostile states and within unstable states that are threatened by civil war, and in the various other roles it plays. Taking an example at random, the UN played a role in securing an agreement on high seas fishing, determining the steps that states may individually take to enforce the agreement and fixing the procedures for settling any disputes between states. The agreed procedures set up in this case, as in many others, involve the International Court of Justice, an important judicial and advisory body established by the United Nations.

There are many bodies that operate in cooperation with the UN or in subordination to it, whose goal is to order the relations between states and thereby help to entrench agreed sovereign liberties. The World Trade Organization, for example, seeks to establish and extend agreed terms of trade among its members. It also hears complaints and imposes penalties on convicted offenders. Another example in the economic and financial domain is the International Monetary Fund, which is meant to foster monetary cooperation, secure financial stability, and promote international trade and prosperity. Yet other examples include the Food and Agriculture Organization, which coordinates efforts to stabilize and ensure food sources; the World Health Organization, which monitors public health around the world; and the International Criminal Court, which was established to guard against the perpetrators of war crimes and other serious offenses escaping justice.

Not only do centralized bodies of these kinds aim, with whatever degree of success, to establish and entrench the sovereign liberties of states. So, somewhat indirectly, do a range

of informal intergovernmental networks of domestic regulatory officials, such as the Basel Committee on Banking Super-
vision; more or less autonomous, influential bodies like the
International Organization for Standardization; and a number
of public–private regulatory regimes (Kingsbury, Krisch, and
Stewart 2005). These combine to impose global regulation
on a variety of activities, commercial and otherwise, defining
and policing the areas where states enjoy entrenched liberties
(Braithwaite and Drahos 2000). They establish international
networks of agencies and officials that have been said to constitute a "new world order" (Slaughter 1997; 2004).

I mean to hold up the bodies and networks listed here as
precedents that show what can achieved on the international
scene, not as ideal models for how things should be done. All of
the examples given are flawed in one way or another. Thus the
arrangement that establishes permanent members of the Security Council of the United Nations, each with a right of veto, is
manifestly objectionable from a republican viewpoint, however
inescapable it may currently seem. The bodies and networks
cited are only meant to show that the recommendations that
our argument would support are not infeasible, building as they
do on what look like fairly robust patterns of development so
far (Ikenberry 2012).

THE SOVEREIGNTY IDEAL AND INTERNATIONAL DEMOCRACY

International bodies of the kind illustrated are needed to establish and entrench the sovereign liberties of representative states
in much the same way that the authorities within a state establish and entrench the basic liberties of citizens. But that obser-

vation immediately raises a problem. What ensures that the bodies introduced to establish the international order will not dominate the very states on which they impose the relevant rules? What guards against domination by the public power that those agencies will inevitably enjoy?[84]

International agencies will not dominate any representative states or their peoples to the extent that they are contestable and controllable by those states. In the domestic sphere, contestability is ensured by making the government collectively contestable in elections, contestable in popular interrogation and protest via the courts, ombudsman bodies, and the media, and contestable by watchdog officials. Contestability in international bodies can be supported electorally by enfranchising member states—or perhaps elected representatives of their peoples (Held 1995)—in the same way. And, even more important, it can be supported by arrangements that parallel domestic contestation of the popular and official varieties.

There is a vital role to be played by international nongovernmental movements in exercising popular contestation and by international review bodies in exercising official contestation. Nongovernmental organizations like Amnesty International, Greenpeace, Oxfam, and Doctors Without Borders can help keep track of how far international agencies live up to the briefs they are given and whether they operate within the constraints imposed. And of course international review bodies, and indeed the reviews that particular states or groups of states can trigger, serve an indispensable function in ensuring that the agencies are held accountable. It is often said that international agencies suffer from a democratic deficit insofar as officials are not popularly elected to office. But this complaint neglects the fact that election is only one way of making authorities accountable. The appointed officials in international agencies and institutions are subject to the constant threat of being called to book, whether as a result of hostile media publicity, hostile NGO criticism, or internal whistleblowers. And that creates a powerful pressure to be faithful to the briefs they are supposed to discharge. Such officials will be able to operate in the service of a personal or sectarian purpose only at considerable peril to themselves.

Our discussion so far supports two lessons: first, that the only hope of institutionalizing the ideal of globalized sovereignty among representative states is by means of international rules and agencies; and second, that this need not raise any special democratic problems, since the states that set them up ought to be capable of controlling such agencies. This puts us in a position to proceed to the second stage of our investigation and discuss the problems raised by states that are impoverished or oppressive and so incapable of representing their peoples. But before moving on, there is one further issue to address.

THE SIGNIFICANCE OF INTER-STATE INEQUALITY

While the states envisaged so far are all representative in character, they are bound to vary enormously in relative population, territory, and resources. This raises two questions. First, is it desirable to impose common rules on states that vary so dramatically, giving them each the same sovereign liberties? And second, assuming it is desirable, is it feasible to expect more powerful states to comply with such common rules?

The peoples of different states will stand no chance of being treated as equals in international negotiation and cooperation—and so no chance of avoiding domination at the hands of other states, for example—unless their representative states are treated as equals. And if their representative states are to be treated as equals in international forums of negotiation, they must enjoy the same sovereign liberties in expressing opinions, making common cause with those of similar interests or opinions, challenging proposals and decisions along accepted lines, and so on. Since states differ in bargaining power, they cannot enjoy equal standing with one another except to the extent that they conduct their deliberations under the norm of norms, as we described it in the last chapter. They cannot seek to drive deals on the basis of what the strong are willing to concede to the weak. They must be prepared to argue for any policies they support, any procedures they recommend, on the basis of considerations that can pass muster on all sides—considerations that all states, large and small, can acknowledge as relevant.[85]

Despite the fact that international negotiation and cooperation is exercised under the influence of the norm of norms, with each party having an equal standing, the varying size of states may still be taken into account. The fact that some states have much larger populations than others, for example, is bound to be pertinent in determining the share of some global goods to which they are entitled, such as the benefits of the attention received from a body like the World Health Organization. And equally, the fact that some states have larger populations than others is bound to be relevant in raising the limits they are allowed to reach in generating global bads: for example, in releasing greenhouse gases into the atmosphere.

I conclude that it is desirable to impose common rules on representative states of different sizes—albeit rules with the kind of flexibility just indicated—offering them each the same sovereign liberties. But is it feasible to expect larger and more powerful states to go along with this? It may well seem not, given that some states may have greater economic wealth, and greater military power, than others. As things currently are, for example, the United States is not only much wealthier than other countries; it spends more on maintaining its military power than most of the rest of the world combined.

Impressed by these differences in wealth and power, we might propose that one superstate should establish an international, benevolent order, acting as the world's police officer; this role has sometimes been ascribed to the United States. Or again, we might propose that a number of states should preserve special powers—as, indeed, within the Security Council of the United Nations—provided that they are goodwilled enough not to interfere with others. Of course, any such proposal is anathema from the republican point of view. It would mean, in effect, that the weaker states could exercise sovereign liberties only by the grace and favor of the stronger. Thus, it is crucial that the sovereign liberties should be entrenched on the basis of an international rule of law that allows no one a special position of power.

But why should a more powerful state not simply throw its weight around in bilateral relations and indeed on international bodies too? Why should we expect a stronger state to go along with the imposition of an order in which it counts as an equal among equals? The issue is important and pressing but it need not prompt outright pessimism.

One of the lessons of recent history is that when a stronger state tries to use hard power, military or economic, to impose on others, the results can be counterproductive. Such power can elicit deep resentment and resistance in those it affects and, having electoral costs, it can undermine the government back home. The experience of the United States in Vietnam or Iraq or Afghanistan bears out the lesson vividly. In each case, the mightiest power on earth undertook what looked like a relatively manageable task and did so with electoral acceptance, even enthusiasm, back home. And in each case, it confronted resentful opposition in the target country and found itself dragged down by waning domestic support and rising domestic criticism.

Another lesson of recent history is that weak states can become a force to reckon with by making common cause with one another and establishing a coalition against the strong. The impact on world trade of the Cairns Group of agricultural producers is an example. Formed in 1986, these agricultural producers had to confront opposition from powerful blocs like the United States, the European Union, and Japan in pushing for the Agreement on Agriculture that was accepted in the Uruguay round of trade negotiations in the mid-1990s. While that agreement did not achieve all that agricultural producers wanted, the ensuing Doha round of negotiations demonstrated the continuing power of weaker states when they act en bloc. This time a group of developing countries was able to stymie the efforts of more powerful states to establish rules that would restrict the trading opportunities open to the weaker.

These observations suggest that the best course for even the strongest states may be to rely on soft, persuasive power, not on the hard, muscle-flexing variety of economic or military might. And if that is right, then there is every reason to think that an arrangement in which countries of different levels of power enjoy the same sovereign liberties, operating under common rules, can prove to be workable as well as attractive.

The inventor of the concept of soft power, Joseph Nye (2004, 5), draws on a range of historical examples in reaching a conclusion that bears out this view:

A country may obtain the outcomes it wants in world politics because other countries—admiring its values, emulating its example, aspiring to its level of prosperity and openness—want to follow it. In this sense, it is also important to set the agenda and attract others in world politics, and not only to force them to change by threatening military force or economic sanctions. This soft power—getting others to want the outcomes that you want—coopts people rather than coerces them.

WHY REPRESENTATIVE STATES SHOULD EXTEND THE SOVEREIGNTY IDEAL

All the points made so far are premised on the assumption that states are representative in character, being effective and non-oppressive agencies that can claim to act in the name of their peoples. But in the real world, some states are too ineffective to discharge some of the basic functions of a state and others are oppressive in nature. So what does the republican viewpoint on international justice entail for a world with states like these?

Imagine for a moment that every people on earth had a representative state to act and speak in its name. In such a world, there would be no reason why states should be concerned with anything other than setting up a system of globalized sovereignty. Each people and state could be indifferent to others and restrict its concern to the welfare of its own citizens. But this is not our world. In ours, some states are impoverished and some are oppressive. And so there is a freedom-based case for why something should be done about the losses to the citizens of such states: for why the peoples in those states should also be effectively incorporated within the global order, and be liberated from poverty and oppression.

It is one thing to say that something should be done about the losses that the peoples of such impoverished or oppressive states suffer. Many people would agree with this statement. But it is quite another thing to say that specific agents or agencies should do it. Prescriptions of this kind can be contentious. I want to argue here that the salient actors who should take on the task of doing something on this front, whether directly or indirectly, are other states, in particular other representative states. They should establish an international order in which such problems of poverty and oppression are effectively addressed.

One argument that might be canvassed for why representative states should take on the required task is that ultimately they are the only agencies with the power to do something effective and that in this case power imposes obligations. As it used to be said that nobles are obliged to help others—*noblesse oblige*—so it may be said in this context that the powerful are obliged to help others: *pouvoir oblige*. But that argument does not carry much weight. Representative states depend for their finances and capacities on the coercive taxation of their citizens and it is not obvious that they should be permitted, let alone obliged, to use those resources for any old cause, however meritorious. If they use those resources in a way that is not warranted by the community-wide standards upheld among their citizens, that forces those citizens into involuntary beneficence, thereby imposing on them in a dominating manner. Such a practice would give the states a Robin Hood role, enabling them to rob the rich at home in order to help the poor and oppressed abroad.

But if this argument does not support the obligation of representative states to support the poor and oppressed elsewhere, other arguments do. All sides in any democratic or half-democratic society, for instance, would valorize the claim that the state should act so as to establish an international order in which its citizens can enjoy security and prosperity. This argues that not only should the state do its bit, in combination with others, to establish the globalized sovereignty we have been envisaging as an ideal for representative states, but also that the state should act in combination with other representative states to relieve poverty and oppression in other regimes, enabling those regimes to assume their place as representative states in a just and stable international order. The citizens of the donor state would stand to benefit, like people everywhere, from any such extension of world order. The extension would increase opportunities for commerce and prosperity and reduce dangers by eliminating potential bases for terrorist networks, for example, and potential breeding grounds for global disease.

This argument for why representative states should assume the obligation to act against poverty and oppression in other states may seem rather self-serving and unedifying. But there is another argument that buttresses it nicely. The citizens of representative states rightly clamor for their own state to do something to cope with the suffering of those elsewhere who are afflicted by outbreaks of famine or violence: the natural evils of tsunamis and earthquakes or the human evils of repression and torture. If representative states are to answer such demands—demands that are presumptively made on the basis of community-wide standards—they are surely entitled to anticipate the demands and devote resources to guarding in advance against the relevant dangers. And that would amount to nothing less than recognizing commitments to the poor and the oppressed elsewhere that require ongoing action, not just action under emergency circumstances.

Most of us believe, of course, that individual human beings do have obligations of justice to help out the needy elsewhere, and when the citizens of a representative state demand that it provide relief for the impoverished or oppressed elsewhere, they are presumably reflecting a sensitivity to such considerations. Those considerations may not directly oblige or even permit a state to provide for justice elsewhere without the authorization of their citizens. But when authorization is forthcoming, it licenses the state to be sensitive to the values involved. It entitles the state in this domain to assume the role of a morally responsive agency.[86]

HOW REPRESENTATIVE STATES SHOULD EXTEND THE SOVEREIGNTY IDEAL

Agreeing that representative states have a duty to be concerned about people who live under ineffective or oppressive regimes says nothing about what exactly they should do in discharging that duty. What are the guidelines, under a republican approach, that ought to direct them in their efforts to combat poverty and oppression?

The first thing to recognize is that there are a number of plausible constraints—constraints grounded in the republican view of things—that the initiatives they adopt should satisfy. No state should be required to act on the international front in a way that sidelines democracy at home; this constraint may not require a referendum on international initiatives, but it does require that decisions be taken on publicly accepted grounds, under publicly endorsed processes. Again, no state should be required to provide assistance for a foreign people that compromises democracy in that country; any assistance furnished should be compatible with the development and maintenance of democratic institutions. And, finally, no state should be required

to provide assistance of a kind that undermines the ideal of globalized sovereignty.

With the possible exception of refugee policy, these constraints
combine to support only responses to impoverishment and
oppression that are taken by a number of states. Only internationally shared assistance is likely to assure those at home that
they are not being coopted into a scheme of one-sided philanthropy. Only such assistance is likely to guard against the dangers of imposing on another people foreign dependency or foreign
government. And only such assistance is likely to keep open the
ideal of a community of states in which each is entrenched in the
enjoyment of a common set of sovereign liberties.

Turning now to the relief of poverty, in particular, what are
the specific duties that might reasonably be imposed on representative states? A good model exists in bodies like the World
Bank and the Food and Agriculture Organization of the UN.
The assistance that these organizations furnish, however inadequate in practice, has two attractive aspects. First of all, it is
aimed at making existing states capable of assuming their own
role in relation to citizens, not at bypassing and subverting those
states; the idea is that the aid should reinforce existing modes of
food production and distribution, not just introduce temporary,
ad hoc substitutes. And second, the multilateral design of the
assistance means that no beneficiary state is put in the debt of a
single benefactor state, being cast in the role of a dependent or
a client; at the very least none is required, as in some bilateral
arrangements, to repay such a benefactor by offering favorable
trade arrangements.[87]

The republican ideal of globalized sovereignty would support
assistance of this state-enabling, multilateral kind, whether provided by international state-sponsored agencies or by nongovernmental organizations such as Oxfam and Doctors Without

Borders, or by a combination of the two. It would argue against bilateral assistance and against assistance that undermines the local government, on the grounds that this is likely in the long run to be a source of domination. Like the assistance of philanthropists in the private arena, such assistance is liable to turn beneficiary countries and peoples into dependents—it is likely to clientelize them, as it is sometimes said—rather than allowing them to make their own way in the international world.

This provides an indication of how we might enrich the ideal of globalized sovereignty to accommodate the need to guard against underdevelopment and poverty in other states. But how should we extend it so that it also provides for assistance against the domination of the peoples who live under oppressive regimes?

What is to count as an oppressive state? The problem is resolved in international practice by recourse to the concept of human rights—if you like, justiciable human rights—that has emerged over the past century or so.[88] Under that practice, a state counts as oppressive just to the extent that it offends against those human rights of its subjects. There are contested accounts of the exact content of justiciable human rights, so that the issue of whether a state has offended against them is still often a matter for interpretation (Forst 2010).[89] But there is certainly broad agreement that many rights count as human rights in the relevant sense. And equally, there is general agreement on the justiciable significance in international relations of alleging that a state has violated the relevant rights of its citizens (Beitz 2009). To establish such a violation is to show that the state is oppressive, as we are using the term, and that its people have a right to expect some form of international vindication. More concretely, it provides what counts on all or most sides as a relevant and good reason, albeit a reason that may not override all other considerations, for the community of states to take punitive or restrictive action.

Determining whether a state counts as oppressive or not pales in difficulty beside the practical problem of determining what the international community should do in the event of deciding that a given regime is oppressive. There are many modes of response, ranging from condemnation to ostracism, economic sanction to military intervention. One issue is to decide which if any of these responses is a plausible candidate, and another is to determine whether the collateral costs of such a response are so high that it is not justified. Those costs will include the dangers and losses imposed by the action on the citizens of the target state, and the dangers and losses for the neighbors of that state and for the states that combine in taking action. Indeed, the costs should also include the fracturing of the international community that may occur as a result of divisions on whether to intervene, as major players—say, the members of the Security Council of the United Nations—take different sides on the issue, thereby jeopardizing possibilities of convergence and action elsewhere.

The costs of acting against an oppressive state are great. They are so great, in fact, that no penalties devised by an international regime of globalized sovereignty are likely to deter all governments from remaining or even becoming oppressive. But this need not be a reason for outright pessimism. No oppressive state can expect to enjoy the effective protection and empowerment that representative states gain under a regime of globalized sovereignty; it will have to rely more on its own resources. And no oppressive state can expect to stand equal with others, on the secure and recognized basis provided by such a regime, thereby achieving a status that is likely to appeal to its people; it will have to nurture its standing with its citizens on more assertive, nationalistic grounds. We may hope that the attractions of full incorporation in the community of sovereign nations can combine with penalties to coax more and more countries to sign up fully to the free international order envisaged here.

THE STRAIGHT TALK TEST

In discussing the requirements of freedom for justice and democracy, we raised the question of what level of equal provision should count as enough. In each case, I offered a working answer. Invoking the eyeball test, I argued that people should each be entrenched against private domination, as justice requires, at a level where everyone by local standards is capable of looking others in the eye without reason for fear or deference. And invoking the tough luck test, I argued that people should be given an equally shared control over a democratic government at a level that enables them to think by local standards that if public decisions go against them, that is just bad luck; it is not the sign of a malign will operating in their lives.

What test might indicate that peoples enjoy equal sovereignty to an acceptably high degree? If there were a regime of globalized sovereignty in place, then it ought to enable peoples—via suitably representative states—to relate to one another in a manner that parallels the way free citizens under a just regime would relate to one another. And equally it ought to enable them to relate to the international bodies and agencies that run the regime in a manner that parallels the way free citizens would relate to a democratic government.

We can capture both requirements in the stipulation that, acting via a representative state—or perhaps via other individuals or bodies—each people in the world ought to be able to address other peoples, and address the agencies it combines

with others to form, as an equal among equals. It ought not to
be required to resort to the tones of a subservient subject and
it ought not to be entitled to adopt the arrogant tones of a master. It ought to enjoy the capacity to frame its expectations and
proposals on the assumption of having a status no lower and no
higher than others and so to negotiate in a straight-talking, open
manner. Each people ought to be able to pass what we might call
the straight talk test.

In discussing the eyeball test, we saw that not only can it
serve to fix the level of entrenchment that people ought to
enjoy in the exercise of their basic liberties, it can also help to
identify the precise set of liberties to establish in a society. A
parallel lesson holds with the straight talk test. In principle,
it can help to guide us in thinking about the exact sovereign
liberties that ought to be entrenched for different peoples. Any
set of liberties that left some in a master's position, others in the
position of servants, would breach this test, undermining the
possibility of reciprocal, inescapably respectful address that it is
meant to encode.

The eyeball and tough luck tests hold out quite high ideals of
justice and democracy—ideals that few regimes actually satisfy.
Equally, the straight talk test holds out a high ideal of international relations that is very far from satisfied in our actual world.
This will become clear when we look at the bottom line, seeking
to compare the republican ideal of a globalized sovereignty of
peoples with other ideals in the area of international justice.

THE BOTTOM LINE

Perhaps the best way to begin situating the republican approach
to international justice is by comparing it with the view that

gained dominance in the seventeenth century, after the West-phalian treaties. The Westphalian view is now well and truly out of fashion, especially since the rise of the human rights movement, but it offers a useful foil for our discussion.

There are three principles associated broadly with the Westphalian orthodoxy, and they pair off nicely with the opposed principles that the republican perspective supports. They are these:

- A state enjoys sovereign freedom just insofar as other states do not actually intervene in the conduct of its domestic business; it need not be secured against intervention.
- The domestic business of a state should not be limited in any way by the international order; what the state does in its own jurisdiction is its own business.
- No people has a right under international arrangements to claim assistance from others, whether in dealing with impoverishment or oppression.

The contrasting republican principles, which are supported by the preceding discussion, offer opposition on every point:

- A state enjoys sovereign freedom just insofar as the international order secures it against other states and global agencies in the exercise of sovereign liberties: choices that are co-enjoyable by all states.
- The sovereign liberties of a state are limited under the international order so as to allow its citizens to enjoy their own individual liberties.
- Every people has a right under the international order to claim assistance from other states in dealing with impoverishment and oppression.

How does the republican ideal of a sovereignty of peoples compare with competitors more contemporary than the West-phalian view? It is distinguished from a range of approaches, broadly cosmopolitan in character, by assuming that representative states have special obligations to their own citizens and do not owe the peoples of other countries in the same way. On the republican view, it is a brute fact that peoples are subject to states that coerce them into obeying the law, as we saw in the last chapter. While states are not obliged to their citizens to reverse that condition, they do have an obligation in freedom to allow those citizens to dictate the terms on which they are coerced; absent such an arrangement, states will be dominating agencies. But states have no obligation of the same kind toward other peoples, since they do not have the same power over them (Nagel 2005).

Not only are states not obliged to treat others as they treat their own citizens, they are obliged to their own citizens not to use taxes to help other peoples except when those citizens explicitly or implicitly demand this, or support it as an implication of a separate demand—say, the demand for an international order. The unqualified, cosmopolitan argument that states have the same duties to other peoples as to their own neglects the fact that states are corporate, coercive bodies and that this argument could support an arrangement of coerced and involuntary philanthropy: an arrangement under which the state, without the say-so of its citizens, uses the money it extracts from them for a goal that is not endorsed under community-wide standards.

One alternative to unqualified cosmopolitanism, variants of which have been pursued by different thinkers (Julius 2006; Valentini 2011), argues that just as the power of the state in relation to its own citizens requires it to pursue democracy and justice for them, so the power that many states and international institutions have over the peoples of other countries—a power that has grown with the globalization of trade and finance—creates an obligation toward those peoples. Different ways of qualifying cosmopolitanism will argue for different policy programs. This general approach can sit fairly happily beside that which is adopted here. Without equating the foreign obligations of states with their obligations toward their own citizens, it would provide an additional reason for being prepared to support provision for those living elsewhere.

But given that they are not cosmopolitan in character, what exactly are the policies that a republican approach would support? The best I can do in giving a sense of the form they are likely to take is to list a number of conditions that every state ought to meet as a good international citizen. While the conditions focus on the performance of a state, they clearly support corresponding policies for the international agencies that states set up and for the nongovernmental agencies that seek to influence and supplement what states can accomplish in the international arena.

The state that counts as a good international citizen:

- ought to be prepared to cooperate with others in committing to the ideal of a sovereignty of peoples—in particular, it ought not to imagine or present itself as special or privileged in any way;
- ought to recognize that in seeking to persuade others about international policies it should only present considerations that all can recognize as relevant, in accordance with the norm of norms;
- ought to abjure any interference in the sovereign liberties of another country and ought to be prepared to play its

part in supporting any internationally approved processes that can be brought with profit against an offending state;

- ought to respect the justiciable human rights of its own subjects—establishing, ideally, an effective democracy—and ought to be prepared to play its part in supporting any internationally approved actions against oppressive regimes;

- ought to seek the help of the international community in the event of failing to be able to provide for its own subjects and ought to be ready to cooperate with other states in providing assistance for countries in such need;

- ought only to favor action against an oppressive regime, or assistance to an impoverished one, that is multilateral in character and avoids clientelizing the recipient country;

- ought to support global arrangements for conserving the planet, preserving the quality of its soil, its water, its climate, its atmosphere, and the other species with which we share it;

- ought to support global arrangements for promoting public goods as well as avoiding public bads, whether in regard to community health, crime prevention, commercial regulation, or simply the promotion of mutual understanding;

- ought to support global arrangements for protecting different peoples against the danger that a multinational body such as a corporation can extract special fiscal or regulatory favors through threats;

- ought to be ready to foster and participate in the various international forums and tribunals, networks, organizations, and agencies whereby such goals and arrangements can be promoted;

- ought to insist on the contestability of these international institutions, guarding against the possibility that they can themselves dominate some states and peoples, having a democratically uncontrolled power of interference;

- ought to protect its people against any residual domination by stronger states, or by international agencies or multinational corporations, by making common cause with states in a similar situation.

The implied requirements on the good state ought to be fairly appealing, at least in light of an appreciation of the republican conception of freedom. They ought not to seem excessively moralistic and utopian, yet they are still very demanding. We need only think about the clientelization of underdeveloped countries by the rich, the arrogance of undemocratic regimes in face of international pressure, and the swagger of powerful governments in supposedly multilateral forums in order to realize that an international world that conformed to republican requirements would be a very different world from ours. Like republican justice and republican democracy, the ideal of republican sovereignty identifies a destination that we can still only dream of attaining, despite the fact that it is manifestly within our collective reach.

EPILOGUE

Whe live in times more uncertain than any our species has faced over the hundred thousand or so years of our existence, and certainly over the twelve thousand years since we began to settle down and till the earth. In the decades and centuries ahead, we will face the prospect of making room for large, perhaps still growing populations in an environment of declining resources, changing climate, and rising sea levels. We may hope for advances in science and technology to help us meet this challenge, but nothing will be more important in enabling us to cope than the social and political arrangements under which we coordinate as individuals and as peoples. If we are to meet the challenges without resort to war and violence—a resort that has plagued us in the sad, stuttering history of our species—then we must find modes of decision-making that answer well to our nature and its needs.

My own view, as I have argued in these pages, is that in the search for a moral perspective on the practices and institutions required in a complex world, the traditional ideal of freedom in the republic may provide the best possible guidance. Freedom is an ecumenical ideal whose relevance to government is recognized on all sides of politics, at least among those who are willing to treat others as equals with themselves. And yet, so I have tried to argue, it is substantive enough under its traditional republican interpretation to direct us decisively in resolving the many questions of justice, democracy, and sovereignty that our world raises.

We need solid empirical research, and good institutional modeling, if we are to be able to offer sensible proposals on how we should reform our different societies or the international arrangements under which our societies relate. But such research and modeling is not enough on its own to direct policy. We also need an ideal by which to orientate in the continuing search for better policy and best practice. In order to meet this need, we can do no better than to rework the ideal of freedom, drawing on the well-tested experience and philosophy of the republic. Republican freedom is certainly not the only good in life but it is a gateway good, as I suggested earlier. Let states look after freedom in this sense and they will look after all that we can feasibly and reasonably charge them with promoting. In particular, they will look after the various concerns that we raised under the headings of social justice, political democracy, and globalized sovereignty.

The very variety of those concerns, however, raises a question that I will address in conclusion. How should the concerns associated with justice, democracy, and sovereignty weigh against one another? How should we weight them in relation to one another when we cannot realize all at once and have to trade off gains on some fronts against losses on others?

If we think of political philosophy as a guide to the best political arrangements or constitutions, on the model of a guide to the world's most livable cities, then various constitutions may seem to score more or less equally in freedom's terms. Under different threats to freedom, more justice may seem to compensate for lesser democracy or sovereignty; more democracy for lesser justice or sovereignty; and even more sovereignty for lesser justice and democracy. But to think in this way, as I suggested, would be to abandon the republican perspective; it would be to cast us as passive consumers in the political realm, not as active citizens.

Things look very different if we think of political philosophy, more appropriately, as a guide to what we can do in politics, alone or together. Under this perspective, democracy makes a natural claim to priority. We can only hope to work for greater justice or democracy in our own societies, or for a fuller enjoyment of sovereignty in the world at large, by advocating suitable policies to our own citizens or to the citizens of other countries. And whatever impact we seek in such public advocacy, we can pursue it without pretension—that is, without pretension to a special knowledge or status—only on the assumption that we can bring others around to our point of view. We can look for it, in other words, only on the assumption that it can secure support in a process where everyone's voice, our own included, is given a hearing (Walzer 1981).

This little book is designed to provide a unified, action-guiding perspective on what we can and should properly seek in politics, and naturally endorses a presumption in favor of democracy. The action it supports is not the vanguardist initiative of a party or clique or religion that would presume to know what people in general want and to claim their authority for its particular aims. The perspective adopted supports action in the marshaling and mounting of popular challenge, not action that leads where the people purportedly ought to follow but may not actually be willing to move.

None of us is entitled to go out and try to change the world all on our own. But change is not impossible, nor despair inevitable. If we embrace the ideal articulated here, we are called to develop the perspective it offers in our own understanding, to share that understanding with those with whom we share our lives, and to try to advance some of its implications in one or another public forum. The forum of choice may be the political party or campaign, the watchdog or pressure group, the town meeting or social movement, the political blog or chat room. It may be the court or tribunal or ombudsman office. Or it may just be the petition to a representative, the letter to a newspaper, the call to a radio talk show. The possibilities are legion in any more or less democratic regime. And, as recent history has testified, there may even be parallel opportunities, however restricted, under regimes of a straightforwardly autocratic character.

Democracy is hard work and, as Oscar Wilde said of socialism, it may even take up too many evenings. But there is much that we can achieve if we use democracy to force government to heed our proposals and objections, grounded as they must be in standards we share across the community. And there is certainly much that we will lose if we abandon the democratic project, forgetting that the price of liberty—and so of justice in all its guises, social, political, and international—is eternal vigilance: that is, a sustained readiness to query and challenge and contest. In the most advanced democracies, there is a host of special interest groups poised to impose their particular will on government by recourse to backroom pressure, financial threat, fraudulent analysis, shameless misinformation, manufactured outrage, drummed-up hysteria—in short, all the motley techniques of intimidation, demagoguery, and deceit. These groups are the enemies of democracy and they can be held at bay only if they are opposed on every front by the public interest activists and organizations on which democratic life relies.

This book is not a political manifesto, but if it has any audience, then the best I could hope for is an audience of those who are democratically committed to taking up this fight—this inevitably continuing struggle—against the usurpation of government by income-heavy, conscience-light elites. I believe that the traditional ideals that this book revives and reworks might be used, however modestly, to fuel the fires of democratic contestation. It is only if those fires continue to burn that we can hope to sustain the refractory and turbulent zeal—the readiness to respond with indignation and purpose to abuses of government—that is the fundamental requirement of a functioning, free republic.

APPENDIX: AN OVERVIEW OF
THE ARGUMENT

The prologue and epilogue of this book—together with the bottom-line sections at the end of each chapter—provide a general guide to the path covered in the course of the argument. But it may help readers to keep track of the argument, particularly when they come back to the book a second or third time—as, of course, I hope they will—to have an overview of how the plot progresses from chapter to chapter. This appendix should also enable new readers to see in outline how the argument goes.

Part 1: The Idea of Freedom

CHAPTER 1: THE PAST AND PRESENT OF FREEDOM

1. In a familiar image from horse-riding, to enjoy free rein in a domain of choice is to be able to act as you wish: to follow your head. But this is not freedom, since it is consistent with someone occupying the saddle and maintaining control. Freedom requires that there be no controller or *dominus*, even one who gives you great latitude or leeway in your choices. In a word, freedom requires non-domination.

2. In the Roman Republic, freedom was taken to require a status that gave you control in your personal affairs—in the exercise of your basic liberties—in relation both to other people and to the law that guarded you against other people; your status was to guard you against private power or *dominium* and public power or *imperium*.

3. This view of freedom was maintained in medieval and Renaissance republican thought and in later republican movements, especially during the English republic in the 1640s and 1650s. It came to be associated with a belief in the need for a mixed constitution—a constitutional division and separation of power—and a citizenry that was willing to monitor and contest government.

4. By the eighteenth century, republican thought had reconciled itself to a constitutional monarchy and become the standard way of thinking about freedom—and the institutional requirements of freedom—in the English-speaking world.

5. Republican ideas primed the revolt of the American colonists against the control that the British Parliament claimed in their affairs: Westminster may have taxed them for only one penny, as Joseph Priestley noted, but it claimed the power to tax them for their last penny. This was an affront to the freedom of the colonists.

6. French republicanism, influenced by the work of Jean-Jacques Rousseau, broke with the Italian-Atlantic tradition in rejecting the mixed constitution in favor of a single sovereign assembly and in casting citizens as participants in government rather than monitors and contestants. It was a distinct, breakaway tradition.

7. While the French development had some impact in dislodging the older republican ideas—including, finally, the

idea of freedom as non-domination—it was the appearance of a wholly new philosophy of freedom, associated with the utilitarian philosopher, Jeremy Bentham, that led to the demise of those ideas in the early nineteenth century.

8. Anxious to extend freedom to all women and workers—and not just to the male citizenry, as had traditionally been the case—Bentham argued that freedom requires just the absence of actual interference, i.e. free rein, not the absence of a power of interference. This made it possible to maintain that women and workers could be free, provided their masters did not actually misuse their power of interference.

9. This new way of thinking fit well with the new industrial world and gave rise to the classical liberal or libertarian perspective. What freedom requires, in this view, is not that the state establish you with the status of an undominated citizen but that it give you protection against outright violence and then leave you to your own devices in working for yourself or in contracting, on whatever terms, to work for another.

10. The classical liberal view gave way in the work of John Stuart Mill to a modern, constitutional liberalism in which material welfare or equality is as important as liberal freedom—that is, freedom as noninterference—and the mixed constitution of republican tradition remains an ideal. This is what liberalism tends to mean in North America, while it often denotes a more libertarian approach in Europe and elsewhere.

11. The republican tradition remains distinctive in emphasizing that freedom requires power against interference, not just the absence of interference. This book argues for this way of thinking—the task in the remainder of part

1–and explores its implications for what overall justice requires: the task of part 2.

CHAPTER 2: FREEDOM WITH DEPTH

1. We look in this chapter at the deep requirements that must be satisfied if you are to enjoy freedom in a choice, arguing for a republican view. (In the next, we look at the breadth of choices in which you must enjoy that deep freedom if you are to have the status of a free republican citizen or person.)

2. The image of freedom developed here answers well, so the argument holds, to our contemporary intuitions about what freedom requires as well as to the long republican tradition. But even more important, as we shall see in part 2, it gives us an ideal of freedom that can ground persuasive theories of social, political, and global justice.

3. To have freedom in a choice between certain options, the first thing needed is that you enjoy the absence of interference, and the presence of capacity, that make it possible for you to enact the option that you actually prefer. In short, you must have the room and the resources to choose as you happen to want to choose.

4. But that is not enough: you must also have the room and resources required for choice, regardless of which option you prefer. Otherwise your freedom to choose would depend on your preferring the right, available option. In a choice with just one available option, you could make yourself free by adapting your preferences so as to prefer it: you could liberate yourself, despite incarceration, by adapting your preferences so as to like being behind bars.

5. Nor are even those two conditions sufficient. You must also enjoy the room and the resources required for choice, regardless of which option others prefer you to choose. Otherwise your freedom to choose would depend on the permission and will of another. Thus, absurdly, you could make yourself free in a certain type of choice—you could give yourself the freedom to vote, for example—not on the basis of any right or power, but just by ingratiating yourself with those who can stop you: say, the employer who might deny you time to go to the polls.

6. This third condition is the core idea among traditional republican writers on freedom. Those authors generally assume that the first two conditions are fulfilled too but, in any case, the fulfillment of those conditions looks to be required for fulfillment of the third. Let those conditions be missing and you will be likely to suffer domination. You will be able to choose whatever option you prefer in a given type of choice—say, speaking out on some issue—only by relying on the good graces of another and thereby exposing yourself to a power of interference on their part.

7. In the republican way of thinking, you do not enjoy freedom here and now in a choice unless you retain the capacity to choose as you wish over certain variations in what you yourself or any others prefer you to choose. But it is not required for your freedom here and now that you retain the capacity to choose as you wish over natural disasters and other contingencies. Subjection to the will of another is more inimical to freedom than exposure to the vicissitudes of nature.

8. The independence from others that is required for republican freedom is consistent with depending for what you can do on the preferences of others on orthogonal matters;

or on the preferences they are constrained to act on by commitments that are more fundamental by received standards; or on preferences they can exercise only so long as you give them the authority or license to do so.

9. What freedom requires is just independence from the unconstrained and unauthorized preferences of others—their voluntary preferences—as to what you or your kind should choose. This status presupposes life in the company of others and demands only that in relevant choices you should be able to choose for yourself; others should not be able to exercise any control over your choice.

10. The domination that takes from your freedom in a choice may be more or less severe, depending on factors such as the degree of interference that others can practice and the degree to which they have a power of imposing it. While it always has a relational aspect, it may also derive from structural features of the culture, economy, or constitution under which you live.

CHAPTER 3: FREEDOM WITH BREADTH

1. In order to count as a free person, it is not enough to enjoy deep freedom—freedom as non-domination—in one or another choice; you must enjoy it over a suitable range of choices. Freedom must be broad as well as deep.

2. The image of the *liber* or free citizen in traditional republican theory, extended to all adult, able-minded, more or less permanent residents—for short, all citizens—suggests that the freedom of the person or citizen requires being secure against the interference of others in the set of choices traditionally known as the fundamental liberties;

more on these below. It means having both the room and the resources required for exercising those choices, regardless of the attitudes of the powerful toward you.

3. The security necessary on this republican image requires both the objective safeguards and supports that can be provided by public laws and the subjective recognition—as a matter of common awareness—that you enjoy that backing. Such laws will typically be supported by social norms. This is to say that as a matter of common awareness, people will each expect the patterns of behavior involved to attract the approval of others and will be reinforced thereby in conforming to them.

4. To sum up, then, the republican ideal of the free person or citizen requires that you enjoy non-domination in such a range of choices and on the basis of such public protection and resourcing that you can stand on a par with others; in those respects you are equal with the best.

5. The set of choices that count as fundamental or basic liberties—the types of choice in which public resourcing and protection is required—can be identified by a ceiling constraint and a floor constraint. The ceiling constraint is that they should include only choices that do not put people at loggerheads, forcing them into competition with one another; the floor constraint is that they should include all the choices that are co-enjoyable in that sense.

6. What set of choices is likely to be co-enjoyable by all? First, people must be able to exercise any one of the choices in the set, no matter how many others are exercising it at the same time; each choice must be co-exercisable. And second, people must be able, so far as possible, to derive satisfaction from the exercise of any choice, no matter how many others are exercising that choice, or any other

choice in the set, at the same time; the set of choices as a whole must be co-satisfying.

7. In identifying a set of choices that meet these conditions and direct us to the sorts of basic liberties the law ought to entrench, we need only focus on upstream choices. One choice is upstream from another if securing it means securing the other, but not vice versa; e.g., securing free speech secures the freedom to speak on a particular topic, and not vice versa. Upstream choices are those co-enjoyable choices that are not downstream from any other co-enjoyable choices.

8. A co-exercisable choice is one that each is individually capable of making and that neither logic nor scarcity prevents others from making at the same time. When scarcity makes a type of choice problematic, as when limited land prevents cowboys and farmers from operating in the same area, conventional rules of property or the like can be introduced to make a circumscribed version of the choice co-exercisable.

9. A co-satisfying set of choices is one in which, ideally, each can derive satisfaction from the exercise of any single choice, no matter how many others are exercising that choice, or any choice in the set, at the same time. The set cannot include choices that inflict harm on others, expose others to domination, or are counterproductive in their effects. Some types of choice may be made co-satisfying by the introduction of suitable rules: although people in an assembly cannot each have the right to speak when they wish, they can have equal rights to speak under Robert's rules of order.

10. Which set of choices is co-enjoyable will vary across societies that differ in technology and culture, but also

across advanced, otherwise similar societies due to reliance on different rules. But the categories involved are familiar: freedom of speech, practice, association, and ownership, for example, as well as the freedom to change employment, move location, and use free time as you wish.

Part 2: The Institutions of Freedom

CHAPTER 4: FREEDOM AND JUSTICE

1. A society is just, on the republican approach, insofar as problems of *dominium* or private power are eradicated, democratic insofar as problems of *imperium* or public power are removed. Justice bears on the horizontal relations between citizens; democracy bears on their vertical relations to government.

2. By every account, justice requires the state to treat its citizens as equals, and by the republican account in particular it requires the state to treat them as equals in providing for their enjoyment of freedom as non-domination. The state must identify a suitably broad set of basic liberties and furnish citizens with the resources and protections necessary for enjoying deep freedom in the exercise of those liberties.

3. This means in the first place that the state should provide a material and institutional infrastructure that is capable of sustaining the arrangement required. The material infrastructure requires secure borders, good means of transport and communication, adequate public spaces, suitable environmental regulation, and the like. The institutional

infrastructure requires a sound legal order, accessible education and training, and the market and investment rules necessary for a flourishing economy.

4. While the republican approach fits with many other approaches in these respects, it emphasizes that the state is essential to sustaining an adequate civil and economic order, rejecting the libertarian idea that that order preexists the state and is more likely to be distorted than nurtured by state regulation and taxation.

5. Justice in the republican image is bound to require, not just an adequate infrastructure for a society of equally free citizens, but also the sort of social insurance that secures individuals and communities at a basic level against the dangers of poverty, illness, and various other forms of vulnerability. Philanthropy cannot meet people's needs adequately since, even when it comes without conditions, it is liable to expose them to dependence and domination.

6. Republican justice requires the insulation of people against the interference of others in their basic liberties, as well as infrastructure and insurance. First, it requires the special insulation of those whose position makes them vulnerable to others, whether to spouses, employers, creditors, those in the cultural mainstream, or the corporate bodies that command a special kind of power.

7. Second, republican justice requires the general insulation of people against crime. On this front, it can address all the questions in a general theory of criminal justice, ranging from what to criminalize, how to pursue surveillance and policing, how to organize prosecution and judgment, and what sorts of penalties to impose on the convicted.

8. What degree of resourcing and protection for people's basic liberties ought a state to seek in pursuit of justice?

The answer proposed here is: that level that by the most demanding local criteria enables people to look one another in the eye, without reason for fear or deference that a power of interference might inspire. This eyeball test allows for a certain inequality but not the sort that would warp people's interaction with one another.

9. The bottom line, spelled out in the text, is a theory of justice that is based on an austere principle—the demands of deep and broad freedom for all—but that argues for a rich and plausible set of demands in what the state should provide for its citizens.

CHAPTER 5: FREEDOM AND DEMOCRACY

1. Assuming that the state is required to protect against private power or *dominium*, how are free citizens to be protected—and protected as equals—against the public power or *imperium* of the state itself? The core republican idea is that if they share equally in controlling the state—if the *demos* or people achieve *kratos* or control—then the legislation, regulation, and taxation of the state will not be dominating; it will be an authorized form of interference of the kind mentioned in chapter 2.

2. Such democratic control of government can only protect people against how the government behaves, of course, not against the fact that people are forced to live in political society, within one or another particular state, and under the coercive imposition of law. Is this a problem?

3. No, it is not. That people are forced to live in political society is not due to a voluntary preference on the part of any state. Nor is the fact that they may have to live in one par-

ticular state or set of states rather than any other; assuming that their own state allows emigration, it is not a voluntary preference but a functional necessity that prompts other states to constrain immigration. Nor is the fact that they have to live under coercive law due to a voluntary preference on the part of their state; assuming that the state has to coerce some citizens into compliance, the requirement to treat citizens as equals requires it to coerce all.

4. The crucial question is whether there are institutions available in principle whereby citizens share equally in controlling their state and the government that runs the state. This is a challenging question, since control requires more than a wayward form of electoral or other influence: it requires the directive sort of influence that imposes a pattern answering to the aspirations of the citizens.

5. There is good reason to think that a system of popular influence has to be indirect or electoral in character, not direct or participatory. But giving everyone the vote will not give people equally shared control. The sticky majority problem means that fixed minorities may be pushed aside on certain issues, the party interest problem that elected representatives may look to their own special concerns in many domains, and the influential lobby problem that those who control the finance and publicity on which politicians depend may often dictate state policy.

6. Making an electoral system into a system of public control requires nonelectoral institutions of a regulatory and contestatory kind that guard against majoritarian oppression of minorities, the exploitation of public office for the electoral or other advantage of incumbents, and in particular the usurpation of state power for purposes of advancing the special interests of the rich and powerful.

7. The envisaged system would have to establish guidelines and agencies to restrict the usurpation of the state by private interests, to create nonelectoral authorities such as the election commission, statistical bureau, or central bank, and to enshrine constitutional and other rules for the protection of minorities. But above all it would have to rely on engaging the public, individually and in social movements, in exercising the eternal vigilance that liberty, by republican tradition, requires.

8. The agents in this system, ranging from appointed officials to self-appointed challengers, are not responsive representatives who channel popular, electorally formed demands. But, arguably, they are indicative representatives of the people, subject to such briefs and constraints in the pursuit of their ends that how they perform in their restricted domains is indicative of what people expect and endorse there. Other indicative representatives that might play an important role in a system of popular control are statistically representative bodies—citizens' assemblies—formed with a view to making recommendations on public policy.

9. The system of popular influence envisaged here, true to the republican tradition, introduces a mixed constitution in which many bodies representative of the people contribute to the exercise of public power and a contestatory citizenry exposes public officials, elected and appointed, to popular interrogation.

10. Could this system of popular, equally accessible influence constitute a system of popular, equally shared control? Not in the sense of giving the preferences of people at any time control over policy—in any case, these preferences are inconsistent and changeable—but perhaps in the sense

of giving commonly accepted standards long-term control over what government does.

11. The system forces the agencies at every node in the system to make their decisions on the basis of considerations or standards that no one who is willing to treat others as equals can deride as irrelevant. This norm of norms outlaws policies that are incompatible with such community-wide standards, and bans any processes for deciding between compatible policies, which are themselves incompatible with the standards.

12. Whether supported in the written constitution or just in established practice, these standards are exemplified by commonly accepted, egalitarian standards that mandate rights of voting and protection for all, that dictate that separate is not equal, and that give women equal status in the public square and in private spaces. They are also illustrated by standards dictating the separation of church and state, the proper order in which public issues should be decided, and the right of areas affected by catastrophe to public assistance.

13. While the various flaws to which democracies are subject can jeopardize the rule of common standards, the evidence of history in both Britain and the United States testifies to the slow democracy whereby such standards can channel and shape public process and policy, thereby helping to establish something approximating an equally shared popular control of the state.

14. What would be required for the democratic control thereby achieved to be sufficient by republican standards? It ought to enable people to satisfy the tough luck test. You ought to be able to think with any public initiative or policy, however unwelcome—say, the decision to build

a prison in your backyard—that it was just tough luck that the decision reached was inimical to your interests; it was not the imposition of an alien, potentially malign will.

15. The bottom line, spelled out in the text, is a theory that gives more importance to democracy than most competitors and that requires much of the democracy it sketches. Democracy has to empower community-wide standards in all aspects of public life and policy, operating on the basis of a system of popular influence that constrains the discretion of government, denies the majority the right to impose on any enduring minority, and contains the power of various elites to exploit or usurp government power in the service of their private interests.

CHAPTER 6: FREEDOM AND SOVEREIGNTY

1. As individuals should not be dominated privately or publicly within their own society, so the peoples that individuals can in principle constitute—ideally, via a state they democratically control—should not be dominated by international bodies: other states, multinational corporations, or international agencies. The domination of a collective people would involve the domination of the individuals comprising it.

2. States that are oppressive or ineffective cannot represent their peoples, whereas states that are not oppressive or ineffective, so we assume, do represent their peoples even if they fail to be fully democratic. The ideal of empowering all peoples—the ideal of globalizing sovereignty—supports recommendations, first, on how representative states should relate to one another and, second, on how

they should behave toward states that fail to be representative of their peoples, whether through being ineffective or oppressive.

3. On the first front, the ideal requires each representative state to enjoy a deep form of sovereignty, in parallel to the deep freedom that individuals require. In whatever choices are authorized—in the sovereign liberties that parallel the basic liberties of individuals—they ought not just to escape the intervention of other bodies: diplomatic, economic, or military. They ought to enjoy the level of entrenchment associated with non-domination, where entrenchment in the case of representative and therefore effective states is likely to require protection only.

4. But what are the sovereign liberties in which they should enjoy such protection? No liberties ought to be authorized that would offend against the freedom of the citizens of those states. But subject to that constraint they ought to include all and only the choices that are co-enjoyable by all states, meeting the requirements of co-exercisability and co-satisfaction.

5. These liberties will often require identification and protection in international law and practice. The identification of the liberties can be achieved via international conventions and covenants, their protection via the international agencies that states set up. Current international arrangements, via the United Nations and similar bodies, already foreshadow the sorts of institutions required.

6. But as representative states ought to be protected against one another—and against other bodies—by international agencies and associated laws, they ought also to have equally shared control over those agencies and laws. There ought to be safeguards against international *imperium* as

well as international *dominium*. This constraint is likely to
be met in good measure insofar as international agencies
are run by the appointees of states and are subject to contestation by official and nonofficial watchdog agencies.

7. This ideal of globalized sovereignty among representative
states and peoples is not utopian. Every compliant state
stands to benefit and the capacity of states to coalesce
against domination means that few if any states, however
strong, can hope to use hard power against others success-
fully: their best hope is often to rely on the soft power of
persuasion and recruitment.

8. Turning now to the second task mentioned, how ought
representative states behave toward the peoples of ineffective and oppressive regimes? Those peoples are entitled
like any people to enjoy their sovereign liberties, under the
republican approach. But are representative states obliged
to promote their freedom in this sense? Are they permitted
to pursue that international goal, relying on the resources
coercively extracted from their own citizens?

9. Yes, on at least two counts. First, community-wide standards in any conceivable representative state will argue for
collaboration with other states in pursuit of a just and sustainable international order. And this goal requires acting
for the liberation of impoverished and oppressed peoples.

10. Second, the citizens of most representative states routinely
clamor for their state to take steps for the relief of impoverished or oppressed peoples whenever an emergency
arises—say, a natural catastrophe or government outrage. And the requirement to respond to such a popular
demand licenses the state to anticipate emergencies and
take preemptive action.

11. The ideal of globalized sovereignty—the international

version of the republican ideal—argues for tight constraints on action for the relief of impoverishment or oppression elsewhere. The action should not undermine democracy at home or abroad and should nurture globalized sovereignty. And in order to guard against introducing domination by the assisting state, any action adopted should be taken on a multilateral basis.

12. When would the international dispensation count as sufficient for delivering the level of non-domination envisaged under the ideal of globalized sovereignty? It would have to enable each people, via its representatives, to enjoy an international counterpart of what the eyeball test and the tough luck test identify as domestic ideals. Intuitively those representatives ought to be able to satisfy the straight talk test, addressing other states and the agents they form in combination with other states without being required to speak in subservient tones and without being entitled to speak in the tones of a superior.

13. The bottom line, spelled out in the text, is a theory of the international order that ought to prevail among peoples that is deeply challenging but still realistic. Its challenges take us well beyond the residual ideal of mutually non-interfering states without forcing us to endorse the utopian vision in which states deny their own citizens any substantive priority and seek cosmopolitan justice for all.

NOTES

1 For debate about this claim, see the exchange involving Ian Carter and Matthew Kramer on the one side, Quentin Skinner and me on the other, in Laborde and Maynor 2007.

2 Operative control may be active or virtual, as this example indicates. I control the horse actively when I use the reins to keep it on a desired path. I control the horse virtually when I let the reins hang loose because the horse is going in the direction I want. This virtual sort of control involves standing by, ready to intervene actively should that be necessary for satisfaction of my wishes.

3 Because those associations are unfortunate, some may prefer a new name for the approach. A good candidate would be "civicism," since the ideal associates freedom with citizenship, both in its historical development and in the form it assumes here. But in this book I shall continue to use the older nomenclature.

4 The recent movement, as I think of it, began from the historical work of Quentin Skinner (1978) on the medieval foundations of modern political thought, and from his subsequent articles in the 1980s on figures such as Machiavelli who wrote within the republican tradition identified by John Pocock (1975). An up-to-date list of English works in neo-republican thought should include these books: Pettit 1997b, Skinner 1998, Brugger 1999, Halldenius 2001, Honohan 2002, Viroli 2002, Maynor 2003, Lovett 2010, Marti and Pettit 2010, MacGilvray 2011; these collections of papers: Van Gelderen and Skinner 2002, Weinstock and Nadeau 2004, Honohan and Jennings 2006, Laborde and Maynor 2007, Besson and Marti 2008, Niederberger and Schink 2013, and a number of studies that deploy the conception of freedom as non-domination, broadly understood: Braithwaite and Pettit 1990, Richardson 2002, Slaughter 2005, Bel-

lamy 2007, Bohman 2007, Laborde 2008, White and Leighton 2008, and Braithwaite, Charlesworth, and Soares 2012. For a recent review of work in the tradition see Lovett and Pettit 2009. This book is naturally built mainly on my own contribution to republican themes. It reflects most closely the work in a recent extended monograph on the republican theory of democracy; see Pettit 2012c.

5 Contemporary republicanism has its origins in the historiographic works of Fink (1962), Robbins (1959), and especially Pocock (1975), which first revived interest in the classical republican writers and charted the historical continuity of their political ideas. Quentin Skinner argued in a number of essays, later collected (and somewhat revised) in Skinner 2002, that these works had failed to recognize that classical republicanism did not endorse a view of freedom as participation in the Rousseauvian mode. And building on this insight, Pettit (1996; 1997b)—and Skinner himself (1998)—cast the republican conception of freedom as one according to which it is the absence of domination or dependence on the arbitrary will of another, and not the absence of mere interference, that matters. This idea of freedom as non-domination has become the crucial unifying theme for those who work within the neo-republican framework, although of course within that frame there are also some differences of emphasis and detail (Pettit 2002b). For a recent, alternative history of thinking about freedom see Schmidtz and Brennan 2010.

6 They also included the republicans who formed the United Irishmen and rebelled unsuccessfully against British rule in 1798. Their leader, Wolfe Tone, signed many of his earlier pamphlets "A Radical Whig." See Cronin and Roche 1973.

7 For a recent view that does not make Rousseau so central, see Israel 2011.

8 Adherents of the Rousseauvian approach may have come to construe freedom in this way under the influence of their opponents. Benjamin Constant (1988) is likely to have had such an impact when, in a famous lecture of 1818, he identified "the liberty of the ancients"—essentially, the liberty hailed by Rousseau—as consisting in the right of playing an equal part in a collectively shared form of self-government. Isaiah Berlin (1969) later described this as a positive conception of freedom.

9 Thomas Hobbes (1994b, 21), arguably, anticipated this development in maintaining that corporal freedom requires only the absence of

obstruction and contractual freedom, as we might call it, the absence of a contracted obligation to another. But Hobbes's views on freedom are notoriously difficult. For commentaries see Pettit 2008a, Skinner 2008, Pettit 2012a, and Skinner 2012.

10 What makes the interference of the law acceptable for Lind? Not the fact that it is subject to the control of the citizenry, as under the republican idea, but the fact, roughly, that it prevents more interference than it perpetrates (70). And on that score, so he thinks, the Americans do quite well, perhaps even better than the British (124).

11 This is unsurprising, since he endorsed the crucial premise in that argument: viz., that "all coercive laws . . . are, as far as they go, abrogative of liberty" (Bentham 1843, 503).

12 Reducing legal constraints on the interference of others may have the effect, of course, of increasing constraints overall, exposing people to the constraining effects of others' actions. Bentham thought that while they themselves took away from freedom, legal constraints would often do more good than harm, reducing constraints overall.

13 They also vary in whether they think that freedom should be understood as a goal to be promoted by social institutions—that is, broadly, in a consequentialist way—or as a constraint on the form that institutions are allowed to take: as a source of natural rights that institutions may not breach. The best example of a natural rights form of liberalism is Nozick 1974. My rendering of republicanism is consequentialist, since I derive the different demands of freedom from the requirement to promote freedom as non-domination as well as possible, treating people as equals. For a defense of this sort of consequentialism, see Pettit 2012b.

14 I am grateful to Cecile Laborde for pressing me to make these distinctions. In previous works I have tended to downplay the distinctiveness of constitutional liberalism, a term I take from her, and have unnecessarily provoked liberal protest; see Christman 1998 and Larmore 2001. One issue I do not address here is how far the commitment to the constitutional forms embraced by this approach is properly grounded in a concern for freedom or equality.

15 See Locke (1960, s 57): "where there is no law there is no freedom," and Kant (1996, 297): "a lawful constitution . . . secures everyone his freedom by laws."

16 For an illuminating account of Rawls's views on freedom see Costa

2009. This argues, contrary to the line taken here, that Rawls comes close to thinking of freedom in terms of non-domination and that his institutional proposals would serve the cause of non-domination quite well.

17 There is no tension between saying that laws and norms constitute freedom, on the one side, and holding on the other that they serve to advance or promote it. As immunity against a disease is not defined by the presence of suitable antibodies, so freedom is not defined by the presence of suitable laws and norms; we can imagine other ways of being immune against the disease and other ways of being proof against the intrusions of others. As we can think of the antibodies doing better or worse in constituting a certain immunity, then, so we can think of laws and norms as doing better or worse in constituting your freedom. And as we may hope for antibodies that do a good job in immunizing us, so we may plan for laws and norms that do a good job in providing us with freedom.

18 In particular, of course, I try to rework the ideas central to the Italian–Atlantic tradition of republicanism, not the ideas associated with the revisionary republicanism—better perhaps the communitarian approach—introduced, as we saw, by Rousseau. I think of a contemporary work like Sandel 1996 as a good example of a communitarian republicanism.

19 In view of the universalizing lesson learned from liberalism, it might not be inappropriate, as some have suggested, to speak of the reworked doctrine as liberal republicanism or republican liberalism (Dagger 1997).

20 Consciously echoing the Roman playwright Plautus, Stephen Sondheim captured these themes nicely in his musical *A Funny Thing Happened on the Way to the Forum*. Pseudolus, a slave, is utterly captivated by the prospect, held out by his master, Hero, of becoming truly free, like "a Roman with my head unbowed"—like a "Roman having rights and like a Roman proud."

21 This assumes that in some relevant sense you enjoy free will, but I ignore the question here of what it is to have free will. I address that question in Pettit and Smith 1996, Pettit 2001c, and Pettit 2001b.

22 This way of interpreting interference contrasts with the approach to the theory of freedom taken by those recent thinkers who, partly with a view to making freedom measurable, restrict interference to

the removal of an option: the prevention of that choice. See Steiner 1994, Carter 1999, and Kramer 2003.

23 Hobbes explicitly defends the view ascribed to him here in his debates with Bishop Bramhall. See Hobbes and Bramhall 1999, 91.

24 As it happens, Berlin fails to recognize that Hobbes is a defender of the view he rejects. Notice that to accept Berlin's view, according to which the freedom of a choice requires that all options be open, is not to deny that you may be said to have chosen something freely even when, unbeknownst to you, the option you chose is the only one you could have chosen. On this issue see Frankfurt 1969.

25 On the importance of robustness, see Pettit 2001a, List 2004 and 2006, and Pettit 2015. For a discussion of robustness and democracy see Southwood 2014.

26 For the record, Berlin (1969, 122) denies the resources element in the first claim too: "Mere incapacity to attain a goal is not lack of political liberty."

27 Another of way of registering the loss of freedom involved here is to notice that, like interference by replacement, it transforms the options you previously had, say in doing X or Y, into options that ought rather to be described as X-if-I-allow-it and Y-if-I-allow-it.

28 The difference of attitude shows up in the fact that we feel warranted resentment at being controlled by another's will but not at being constrained by factors that have nothing to do with will; here we are entitled only to feel exasperation. Indeed, we do not feel warranted resentment just at the ill will of others, as suggested in Peter Strawson's (1962) classic paper "Freedom and Resentment." We may also resent the fact that others have the power to subject us to their ill will. This resentment presupposes that something can be done to change things, of course, and it will be warranted if it is directed at parties who can rectify the situation—say, the government—or if it is directed at the powerful themselves insofar as they take their power for granted, do not do anything to renounce it, or take positive pleasure in exercising it.

29 When the bank acts on the general policy, imposed by local standards, that constrains how it treats you, whether well or badly, it acts involuntarily in the sense identified by Serena Olsaretti (2004). On her approach, acting on a preference will be involuntary—as in giving the robber your money rather than losing your life—insofar as there is no acceptable alternative to enacting that preference.

30　And equally, of course, the impact on freedom is intuitively worse when the interference involved affects a preferred option rather than an unpreferred option.

31　There is a considerable literature on the measurement of freedom, particularly in economic circles, but most approaches do not distinguish between these two different dimensions; see Sugden 1998. For an example and defense of such an approach, see Carter 1999. Carter tries to cast all offenses against free choice as acts that prevent choice, removing one or another option, as do Steiner (1994) and Kramer (2003). For an exchange between their viewpoint on freedom and the republican alternative, see Laborde and Maynor 2007.

32　The notion of a social norm that is introduced here picks up points made in a variety of approaches. See, for example, Hart 1961, Winch 1963, Coleman 1990, Sober and Wilson 1998, Elster 1999, and Shapiro 2011.

33　Norms, as I describe them here, may or may not be internalized: people may or may not actually approve or disapprove on the pattern that others expect them to follow. Equally, norms may or may not be generally propounded by individuals as norms that the group endorses. For a discussion of such matters see Pettit 2015.

34　This plausible story is borne out by the evidence that most people obey the law not for fear of punishment, but on the basis that social norms put lawbreaking off the menu of acceptable options. See Tyler 1990.

35　We shall see later in the chapter that the basic liberties have to be carved out by law; they are not a natural kind. This means that there may be a policy issue in many cases between reducing the scope of some basic liberties in order to increase the number of basic liberties available and expanding the scope of those liberties at a cost to the number available overall. While I ignore that issue here, the general approach would suggest that it is best decided on the basis of what best facilitates satisfaction of the eyeball test introduced in the next chapter.

36　What is the level of assistance—say, assistance for the disabled—that a society ought to provide? The issue is best settled by reference to the eyeball test.

37　That observation raises a question in turn. Should we entrench choices that are not available to individuals in this way but are accessible to groups of people who have voluntarily associated with one another, as when they have incorporated as a church or company or club? In general, I think we should avoid entrenching any group choices whose entrenchment does not follow from the entrenchment of certain individual choices. Going further in entrenching group freedoms is liable to empower certain coalitions and to impact negatively on the freedom of individuals outside those coalitions.

38 The farmer and the cowboy will be familiar from Rogers and Hammerstein's musical *Oklahoma!*, but the predicament they exemplify was already a matter of human experience in clashes between farming and foraging peoples, as early as the fifth millennium BCE; see Morris 2010, 112–14, 127–28, 271.

39 While this conception of the citizenry is broad in one respect, of course, it is narrow in another; it does not include children or those suffering, permanently or temporarily, from cognitive or associated limitations or ailments. This means that the discussion in this chapter ignores issues of justice in relation to children and the intellectually disabled.

40 Kant is a figure, with roots in the republican tradition, who particularly emphasized the need for a state and a law in order to give people freedom in respect of ownership. See Ripstein 2009 and Stilz 2009.

41 Is this view in conflict with John Locke's (1960) famous claim that property exists in the state of nature and that the principal role of the state is to judge and regulate conflicts over property and related matters? Not necessarily. Locke's state of nature can be conceived of as a condition in which norms have emerged and gained a hold on people's mutual expectations but have not yet been reinforced by state-imposed laws or indeed state-imposed adjudication and sanction. In that conception, it is a protopolitical regime, not a regime that is strictly prepolitical. It resembles H. L. A. Hart's (1961) conception of a condition in which the primary rules of coordination apply but have not yet been supported by the secondary rules of recognition, adjudication, and enforcement that the state introduces.

42 Although philanthropy will be unsatisfactory in republican terms, of course—although it will not provide people with freedom as non-domination—it will be a much better alternative than outright neglect.

43 One argument against compulsory public insurance, and for discretionary private philanthropy, might seem to be that personal problems are often self-induced. What if the people who suffer problems

are to blame for falling on bad times; they gambled their money away, they smoked excessively or drove recklessly, or they engaged in legally risky ventures (Dworkin 2000; Fleurbaey 2008)? Isn't there a certain moral hazard in providing for public insurance against an event for which a person holds a certain responsibility? Might it not lead to reckless risk-taking? It might but it probably wouldn't, for two reasons. First of all, the crises involved are such that few would willingly run a salient risk of suffering such a problem. And second, the insurance benefits available are not likely to be such as to compensate fully for the loss endured in such a crisis.

44 This policy would run directly counter to "the traditional negative libertarian 'at-will' doctrine that, consistent with contractual obligations, an employer may fire an employee for 'good cause, no cause or even for cause morally wrong'" (Levin 1984, 97). For historical background see Cornish and Clark 1989, 294–5. My support for restrictions on the ability of employers to fire at will presupposes a less than fully competitive market. For a fine and congenial discussion of the market implications of republicanism in more ideal circumstances, see Taylor 2013. On the history of republican attitudes to markets, see MacGilvray 2011.

45 This means that effective action against the possibility of corporate abuses needs international action. The good news on that front, although it is news only about a first step, is that in 2011 the United Nations Human Rights Council adopted the rules proposed by the Special Representative of the Secretary General, John Ruggie, for applying human rights law to corporations. See Knox 2011.

46 For an argument that the pattern is not absolutely universal and that there is a variety in criminal justice, corresponding to the variety in capitalist organization (Hall and Soskice 2001), see Lacey 2008.

47 Other authors have recently emphasized the importance of interactional equality of this kind; see Anderson 1999, Scheffler 2005, and O'Neill 2008.

48 Even John Stuart Mill (2001) suggests that a society should seek to reduce the attractions of choices that can threaten long-term damage to the chooser by imposing relatively higher taxes on the resources that the choices require.

49 The first liberty-centered principle is meant to have priority in the sense, roughly, that its satisfaction cannot be sacrificed in any degree for the sake of the greater satisfaction of the second.

50 I ignore the fact that Rawls's basic liberties, unlike those envisaged here, include procedural liberties such as the freedom to stand for office and vote. I do not see those as liberties in the sense that is relevant to justice but as rights that are related rather to the requirements of democracy, to which I turn in the next chapter. Rawls merges concerns about the horizontal relations between people and concerns about their vertical relations to government, whereas I think that clarity is best served by keeping them apart: it flushes out the issue, discussed in the epilogue, of which of these relations should be given primacy in political philosophy and advocacy.

51 For a good recent interpretation and defense of luck egalitarianism, see Tan 2008. For a response that I find congenial, see Sanyal 2012.

52 Of course, the basic structure to be chosen in Rawls's view includes certain procedural liberties such as the liberty to vote or to stand for office, as we have seen. But these procedural liberties tend to get downplayed—they are not given the importance that republicanism gives democratic devices in general—and he even casts them as "subordinate to the other freedoms" (Rawls 1971, 233).

53 Notice that an order established in that way would not itself be dominating, since it would not impose anyone's will on others; the norms would operate as blindly and blamelessly as a force of nature.

54 The evidence cited in Pinker 2011 bolsters this claim, since it strongly suggests that in the absence of the coercive state, levels of violence are likely to be higher by many orders of magnitude.

55 For an elaboration of the commitment in democracy to equality, see Christiano 1996 and 2008.

56 Most historical republican thinkers did not make use of the term "democracy," even when it came into vogue in the early modern period. This, I suspect, is because absolutist opponents like Bodin and Hobbes had given an unwelcome meaning to the word, treating it as rule by an absolute, majoritarian assembly and contrasting it with the mixed constitution.

57 Equally, of course, an undemocratic regime might impose laws that are just, albeit not robustly or securely just. A colonial administration would be the very paradigm of an undemocratic regime but might establish a just social order. In such a case, we would have no obligation not to try to overthrow the system, even though we would have an obligation to honor and preserve the laws.

58 What democracy ensures, on this account, might be described as

legitimacy; see Pettit 2012c. While he would not endorse my particular way of making the distinction, the person who has done most to underline the distinctive character of legitimacy is A. J. Simmons (1976; 1979; 1999). Some authors treat legitimacy as a halfway house to justice, as when Ronald Dworkin (2011, 321–22) argues that a state which seeks justice counts as legitimate, even if it does not achieve it. A much larger number follow Kant—and, in most cases, Rawls (1993, 224)—in taking legitimacy to consist in a contractual form of justice: that is, justice construed as justifiability to citizens in suitably public terms. This group includes Thomas Nagel (1991), T. M. Scanlon (1998), Brian Barry (1995), Rainer Forst (2002), Charles Beitz (1989), and Thomas Pogge (1990). For a critique see Simmons 1999.

59   I ignore here the role of the monarchomach (or king-killing) tradition of thought as that is represented, for example, in the late sixteenth-century tract *Vindiciae Contra Tyrannos* (Languet 1994). This argued against absolutists that any people that is ruled by a monarch must be supposed, as a collectivity, to have made a contract with their ruler under provisos that would allow them to dismiss that ruler—literally or figuratively to kill the king—in the event of certain forms of injustice or tyranny.

60   This contractualist approach was adopted by different thinkers out of a variety of motives: conservative, reformist, and revolutionary. The motive of one of its earliest and most influential sponsors, Thomas Hobbes (1994b; a; 1998), was to establish, as he thought he could establish, that it would have made uniquely good sense in the state of nature for people to opt for a sovereign with absolute power; no other possibility, he thought, was open. The motive of John Locke (1960), a later seventeenth-century thinker, was to argue that, on the contrary, in the state of nature properly conceived, the motive to form political society would only have supported giving government a conditional power: a power that was conditional on its discharging presumptive duties, where a failure to do so would justify majority revolt. And the motive of the renegade eighteenth-century republican Jean-Jacques Rousseau (1997) was to show that in the state of nature, as he thought of it, people would only be justified in agreeing to form a regime where they could each play an equal participatory part; they would each be a voting member of

a collective legislature, where decisions are taken on the basis of a majority vote.

61 But might the collection of states in the world as a whole, if not your particular state, count just by virtue of its existence as a dominating presence in your life? There are two things to say about this possibility. First, the existing collection of states is not a group agent with the capacity to form and act on a single will—it is not organized in the fashion of a corporation or church or one of its member states (List and Pettit 2011)—and does not have a will to impose. Second, even if that collection morphed into a world state, constituting a group agent, it is possible that it might not count as dominating just in virtue of imposing a political order. The need for it to keep the peace, treating individuals as equals, might constrain it under accepted views of the role of a state to stay in existence and continue to operate. Whether or not it was dominating, then, would depend on whether it was democratic in its character and organization.

62 In these cases, the second element is not strictly necessary for the absence of domination. Even if the exercise of the power—the interference practiced—were not otherwise under the control of the interferees, the fact that they could set aside the arrangement at will would make for a certain sort of control; it would give them the power of exit.

63 I may exert influence in a virtual rather than an active fashion. Riding a horse, I exert active influence when I pull on the reins to affect the direction of the horse but I exert virtual influence when I let the reins hang loose because the horse is already going in the desired direction. Both forms of influence may implement operative control, which contrasts with merely reserve control. I assume here that reserve control is not enough for democracy.

64 Even under a system of compulsory voting such as that in Australia, people may spoil their ballot and are in no sense compelled to have a normal electoral input. But it is worth noticing that even when people do not vote—or do not contest government decisions in any active way—still they exercise some influence: they reduce the majority of the winning party or they allow government not to have to deal with their contestation. On such matters see Guerrero 2010.

65 For a defense of both the necessity and the sufficiency of such a majoritarian regime, see Waldron 1999b and 1999a.

66 This claim is defended by democratic theorists across a wide spectrum. See, for example, Shapiro 2003.

67 When those who seek to exercise influence over a range of outcomes divide into winners and losers on any issue—when it is not a case where everyone's contribution has some effect on the direction taken—then a reasonable metric of influence is given by the chance of being on the winning side in any randomly selected outcome. For a discussion of related issues, see Tuck 2008.

68 For a recent exploration and defense of Machiavelli's commitment to radical democracy in broadly this sense, see McCormick 2011.

69 The norm of norms, as I call it, reflects the pressures of interpersonal deliberation tracked classically by Habermas (1984, 1989). For a helpful commentary see Elster 1986. The idea is central, as I go on to mention, in the tradition of deliberative democracy.

70 This is how Will Kymlicka (1995) argues, for example, in favor of certain multicultural arrangements.

71 Or, I should add, under a process that is selected by a process that community-wide standards support, or even by a process that is selected by a process that community-wide standards support, or . . . The addition is necessary in order to cope with the difficulty that as there may be a number of candidate policies that fit with accepted standards, so there may be a number of candidate processes that do so too. In most cases, of course, a plausible, community-wide standard may be to follow precedent in contested cases, and this is liable to select a unique process as the one to be followed.

72 To return to a theme in earlier notes, they implement an operative form of control over government via a virtual as distinct from an active form of influence. They control government in the way I control a horse when, finding that the horse is going in the direction I want, I let the reins hang loose; this is distinct from giving the horse free rein, since I remain ready to pull on the reins should the horse take an undesired turn.

73 The thought also applies in the case where they find themselves charged with a crime, convicted, and sentenced to some hard treatment. If they were guilty, then they have only themselves to blame and it was tough luck in a special sense that they were caught. If they were not guilty, and the system really is generally reliable, then it was tough luck that the appearances pointed misleadingly to their

guilt. While it is strange to say that a duly convicted prisoner would remain free—that is, retain the status of a free person—under a democratic regime of the kind envisaged here, it is worth remembering that crediting such a prisoner with freedom marks a salient and useful contrast to the prisoner of a lawless, dominating regime.

74 There are some self-described liberal writers, however, who argue that the cause of freedom is tied up with the cause of democracy, though only as a matter of institutional, not conceptual necessity; see, for example, Holmes 1995 and Richardson 2002. Another author who argues for such a connection, though not in the name of liberalism, is Habermas (1995).

75 Defenses of such positions can be found, for example, in Beitz 1989, Cohen 1989, Christiano 1996, and Estlund 2007.

76 I ignore the fact that a body of individual representatives, by any given criterion of representation, may not constitute a representative agent; the aggregation of its decisions may introduce too much noise to preserve the representative relationship. For further discussion, see Pettit 2012c.

77 For a closely related, republican theory of international justice see Laborde and Ronzoni 2012; among other features, this offers a succinct account of the pathologies of the current international order that a republican theory would indict. For a more cosmopolitan use of republican theory, see Bohman 2007.

78 This is to say that the argument presupposes a normative individualism: the view that it is only the interests of individual human beings, not the interests of any agencies or bodies that they create, which should dictate political arrangements. See Kukathas and Pettit 1990, and List and Pettit 2011 and 2012.

79 In structuring the issues in this way, I follow broadly the pattern established by John Rawls (1999) in his *Law of Peoples*. The chapter builds on work done elsewhere; see Pettit 2006, 2010c, and 2010a.

80 One reason for thinking that a non-oppressive, effective state will act and speak for its people is the following: if a regime is not oppressive, then it must allow freedom of expression and association; and if it allows these freedoms, then community-wide standards are likely to emerge among the populace and, even in the absence of electoral institutions, to have a shaping impact on government performance.

81 Still, it might be said, it is one thing to have a world of many states, but quite another to have a world with states established on the cur-

rent boundaries. Why not opt for a world with states that are better paired off with culturally harmonious groupings? Insofar as a state works well, it will give unity and harmony to the people who organize themselves through it. But it is scarcely deniable that things might generally go better under a revised set of state–people pairings and, in some critical cases, that current pairings require urgent attention. Notwithstanding those facts, however, I shall assume in what follows that states maintain the identities they have in the current world. If we were to drop that assumption, so much would be up for grabs that there would be little we could prescribe with any confidence.

82 Although there is no difference in the sorts of obligations that states owe to their own citizens and to foreigners, on this approach, there may be differences in the demands that those obligations impose in the two areas. The demands on a state will be a function, not just of the obligations in which they are grounded, but also of the potential effectiveness of its interventions. On some interpretations, it should be noted, the authors represented here as cosmopolitans may endorse the qualified form of cosmopolitanism mentioned in the final section of the chapter. For a broadly congenial alternative to cosmopolitanism, see Cohen 2012.

83 This is particularly so with democratic states. As individuals seek approval and shrink from disapproval, so in general we may expect them to shrink from the disapproval, and to bask in the approval, that their country earns on the international scene. And so we can expect them, under a more or less democratic regime, to pressure and police their country into conforming to accepted standards.

84 One response to this problem might be to say that whereas individuals do not have the option of exiting from states, states do have the option of exiting from international treaties and organizations. That exit option means, so it may be said, that there is not the same problem of public domination in the international sphere that there is in the domestic (Hirschman 1970). But this comment is not persuasive. While it may be true that states retain the formal right of departing from any of the international arrangements they enter, this formal right will often not amount to very much, since the cost of exit is likely to be prohibitive. Departing the arrangement would mean incurring the displeasure of other members of the organization and those others will inevitably have the opportunity to impose penal-

ties, as well, indeed, as the incentive to do so: imposing penalties would guard against the prospect of further defections.

85 The enforcement of such international equality may not seem fair, as it may be said that the citizens of smaller states will be able to have a deeper impact on what is done in negotiation by their representative states than the citizens of larger states. But under the model of democratic control that we developed in the last chapter, this need not be so. The impact of citizens on their state is determined by the impact of the community-wide standards they uphold, and the depth of this impact may not be sensitive to variations in the number of citizens. But even if there were an unfairness involved here, it would reflect a fault in the organization of the larger states—after all, they could federate or even divide into smaller states—not a fault in the structure of international relations.

86 That the foreign obligations of a representative state are of a different kind from its obligations to its own citizens does not strictly entail that they are obligations that inevitably require less than domestic obligations. For all we have said, the requirement on representative states to protect others against impoverishment or oppression may occasionally impose more onerous duties than the requirement to look after their own citizens.

87 Multilateralism in international action serves the same sort of role as the mixed constitution in domestic matters; it guards against power lying in the hands of just one state, as the mixed constitution guards against it lying in the hands of one domestic individual or body.

88 Over the past century or so, states that abuse their own subjects— and the abuses are equal to the worst in history—have become increasingly exposed to external publicity and reprobation, due to the development of an international press and other media. At the same time, other states have been subjected to pressure from their own subjects to do something about such abuses, due to the development of more democratic regimes. And in a world with growing commercial and financial linkages, and with more and more international agencies, there are new initiatives that states may combine to take against an abusive state. Apart from military intervention, the principal weapons in the new arsenal include condemnation, ostracism, and the use of economic sanctions. It is in the context of such developments that the concept of human rights has emerged as a

way of identifying cases where such weapons may reasonably be employed by the international community.

89 Crucially, of course, the mere fact that a regime is not democratic will not make it oppressive. Thus, by most accounts, there is no human right to democracy (Cohen 2006).

REFERENCES

Anderson, E. 1999. What Is the Point of Equality. *Ethics* 109:287–337.

Appiah, K. A. 2010. *The Honor Code: How Moral Revolutions Happen.* New York: Norton.

Atiyah, P. S. 1979. *The Rise and Fall of Freedom of Contract.* Oxford: Oxford University Press.

Bakan, J. 2004. *The Corporation: The Pathological Pursuit of Profit and Power.* New York: Free Press.

Barry, B. 1995. *Justice as Impartiality.* Oxford: Oxford University Press.

Beitz, C. R. 1979. *Political Theory and International Relations.* Princeton: Princeton University Press.

———. 1989. *Political Equality: An Essay in Democratic Theory.* Princeton: Princeton University Press.

———. 2009. *The Idea of Human Rights.* Oxford: Oxford University Press.

Bellamy, R. 2007. *Political Constitutionalism: A Republican Defense of the Constitutionality of Democracy.* Cambridge, UK: Cambridge University Press.

Bentham, J. 1843. Anarchical Fallacies. *The Works of Jeremy Bentham, Vol. 2.* Ed. J. Bowring. Edinburgh: W. Tait.

Berlin, I. 1969. *Four Essays on Liberty.* Oxford: Oxford University Press.

Besson, S., and J. L. Marti. 2008. *Law and Republicanism.* Oxford: Oxford University Press.

Bohman, J. 2007. *Democracy Across Borders: From Demos to Demoi.* Cambridge, MA: MIT Press.

Braithwaite, J. 2002. Setting Standards for Restorative Justice. *British Journal of Criminology* 42:563–77.

Braithwaite, J., H. Charlesworth, and A. Soares. 2012. *Networked Governance of Freedom and Tyranny: Peace in East Timor.* Canberra: ANU Press.

Braithwaite, J., and P. Drahos. 2000. *Global Business Regulation.* Cambridge, UK: Cambridge University Press.

Braithwaite, J., and C. Parker. 1999. Restorative Justice is Republican Justice. In *Restorative Juvenile Justice.* Ed. G. Bazemore and L. Walgrave. New York: Willow Tree Press.

Braithwaite, J., and P. Pettit. 1990. *Not Just Deserts: A Republican Theory of Criminal Justice.* Oxford: Oxford University Press.

Brennan, G., and P. Pettit. 2004. *The Economy of Esteem: An Essay on Civil and Political Society.* Oxford: Oxford University Press.

Broome, J. 2012. *Climate Matters: Ethics in a Warming World.* New York: Norton.

Brugger, W. 1999. *Republican Theory in Political Thought: Virtuous or Virtual.* New York: Macmillan.

Burke, E. 1970. *The Philosophy of Edmund Burke.* Ann Arbor, MI: University of Michigan Press.

Caney, S. 2005. *Justice Beyond Borders: A Global Political Theory.* Oxford: Oxford University Press.

Carter, I. 1999. *A Measure of Freedom.* Oxford: Oxford University Press.

Christiano, T. 1996. *The Rule of the Many: Fundamental Issues in Democratic Theory.* Boulder, CO: Westview Press.

———. 2008. *The Constitution of Equality: Democratic Authority and Its Limits.* Oxford: Oxford University Press.

Christman, J. 1998. Review of Philip Pettit, *Republicanism: A Theory of Freedom and Government. Ethics* 109:202–6.

Cicero, M. T. 1998. *The Republic and The Laws.* Oxford: Oxford University Press.

Cohen, G. A. 1993. Equality of What? On Welfare, Goods, and Capabilities. In *The Quality of Life.* Eds. M. C. Nussbaum and A. Sen. Oxford: Oxford University Press: 9–29.

Cohen, J. 1989. Deliberation and Democratic Legitimacy. *The Good Polity.* Eds. A. Hamlin and P. Pettit. Oxford: Blackwell: 17–34.

———. 2004. Minimalism About Human Rights: The Most We Can Hope For. *Journal of Political Philosophy* 12:190–213.

———. 2006. Is There a Human Right to Democracy? In *The Egalitarian Conscience: Essays in Honour of G.A.Cohen.* Ed. C. Sypnowich. Oxford: Oxford University Press.

Cohen, J. L. 2012. *Globalization and Sovereignty: Rethinking Legality, Legitimacy amd Constitutionalism.* Cambridge, UK: Cambridge University Press.

Coleman, J. 1974. *Power and the Structure of Society.* New York: Norton.

———. 1990. *Foundations of Social Theory.* Cambridge, MA: Harvard University Press.

Constant, B. 1988. *Constant: Political Writings*. Cambridge, UK: Cambridge University Press.

Costa, M. V. 2009. Rawls on Liberty and Domination. *Res Publica* 15:397–413.

Cronin, S., and R. Roche. 1973. *Freedom the Wolfe Tone Way*. Tralee: Anvil.

Dagger, R. 1997. *Civic Virtues: Rights, Citizenship, and Republican Liberalism*. Oxford: Oxford University Press.

Dryzek, J. S. 1990. *Discursive Democracy: Politics, Policy and Political Science*. Cambridge, UK: Cambridge University Press.

Duff, R. A. 2001. *Punishment, Communication, and Community*. Oxford: Oxford University Press.

Dworkin, R. 1978. *Taking Rights Seriously*. London: Duckworth.

———. 1986. *Law's Empire*. Cambridge, MA: Harvard University Press.

———. 2000. *Sovereign Virtue: The Theory and Practice of Equality*. Cambridge, MA: Harvard University Press.

———. 2011. *Justice for Hedgehogs*. Cambridge, MA: Harvard University Press.

Elster, J. 1986. The Market and the Forum: Three Varieties of Political Theory. In *Foundations of Social Choice Theory*. Ed. J. Elster and A. Hillard. Cambridge, UK: Cambridge University Press.

———. 1999. *Alchemies of the Mind: Rationality and the Emotions*. Cambridge, UK: Cambridge University Press.

Ely, J. H. 1981. *Democracy and Distrust: A Theory of Judicial Review*. Cambridge, MA: Harvard University Press.

Eskridge, W. N., Jr., and J. Ferejohn. 2010. *A Republic of Statutes: The New American Constitution*. New Haven: Yale University Press.

Estlund, D. 2007. *Democratic Authority: A Philosophical Framework*. Princeton: Princeton University Press.

Ferguson, A. 1767. *An Essay on the History of Civil Society*. Edinburgh: Millar and Caddel (reprinted New York: Garland, 1971).

Fink, Z. S. 1962. *The Classical Republicans: An Essay in the Recovery of a Pattern of Thought in Seventeenth-Century England*. Evanston, IL: Northwestern University Press.

Fishkin, J. 1991. *Democracy and Deliberation: New Directions for Democratic Reform*. New Haven: Yale University Press.

———. 1997. *The Voice of the People: Public Opinion and Democracy*. New Haven: Yale University Press.

Fleurbaey, M. 2008. *Fairness, Responsibility and Welfare*. Oxford: Oxford University Press.

Foner, E. 1970. *Free Soil, Free Labor, Free Men: The Ideology of the Republican Party Before the Civil War.* Oxford: Oxford University Press.

Forst, R. 2002. *Contexts of Justice: Political Philosophy beyond Liberalism and Communitarianism.* Berkeley: University of California Press.

———. 2010. The Justification of Human Rights and the Basic Right to Justification: A Reflexive Approach. *Ethics* 120:711–40.

Frankfurt, H. 1969. Alternate Possibilities and Moral Responsibility. *Journal of Philosophy* 66:829–39.

Fukuyama, F. 2011. *The Origins of Political Order: From Prehuman Times to the French Revolution.* New York: Farrar, Straus and Giroux.

Gaus, G. F. 1983. *The Modern Liberal Theory of Man.* London: Croom Helm.

Goodin, R. E., and S. R. Ratner. 2011. Democratizing International Law. *Global Policy* 2: 241-47.

Guerrero, A. 2010. The Paradox of Voting and the Ethics of Political Representation. *Philosophy and Public Affairs* 38:272–306.

Gutmann, A., and D. Thompson. 1996. *Democracy and Disagreement.* Cambridge, MA: Harvard University Press.

Habermas, J. 1984, 1989. *A Theory of Communicative Action.* 2 vols. Cambridge, UK: Polity Press.

———. 1995. *Between Facts and Norms: Contributions to a Discourse Theory of Law and Democracy.* Cambridge, MA: MIT Press.

Hall, P. A., and D. Soskice, eds. 2001. *Varieties of Capitalism: The Institutional Foundations of Comparative Advantage.* Oxford: Oxford University Press.

Halldenius, L. 2001. *Liberty Revisited.* Lund, Sweden: Bokbox.

Hart, H. L. A. 1961. *The Concept of Law.* Oxford: Oxford Unviersity Press.

———. 1973. Rawls on Liberty and its Priority. *University of Chicago Law Review* 40:534–55.

Hayward, C. 2011. What Can Political Freedom Mean in a Multicultural Democracy? On Deliberation, Difference and Democratic Government. *Political Theory* 39:468–97.

Held, D. 1995. *Democracy and the Global Order: From the Modern State to Cosmopolitan Governance.* Stanford: Stanford University Press.

Hill, L. 2000. Compulsory Voting, Political Shyness and Welfare Outcomes. *Journal of Sociology* 36:30–49.

Hirschman, A. O. 1970. *Exit, Voice, and Loyalty: Responses to Decline in Firms, Organizations, and States.* Cambridge, MA: Harvard University Press.

Hobbes, T. 1994a. *Human Nature and De Corpore Politico: The Elements of Law, Natural and Politic.* Oxford: Oxford University Press.

———. 1994b. *Leviathan.* Ed. E. Curley. Indianapolis: Hackett.

———. 1998. *On the Citizen.* Ed. and trans. R. Tuck and M. Silverthorne. Cambridge, UK: Cambridge University Press.

Hobbes, T., and J. Bramhall. 1999. *Hobbes and Bramhall on Freedom and Necessity.* Ed. Vere Chappell. Cambridge, UK: Cambridge University Press.

Holmes, S. 1995. *Passions and Constraint: On the Theory of Liberal Democracy.* Chicago: University of Chicago Press.

Honneth, A. 1996. *The Struggle for Recognition.* Cambridge, MA: MIT Press.

Honohan, I. 2002. *Civic Republicanism.* London: Routledge.

Honohan, I., and J. Jennings, eds. 2006. *Republicanism in Theory and Practice.* London: Routledge.

Husak, D. 2008. *Overcriminalization.* Oxford: Oxford University Press.

Ikenberry, G. J. 2012. The Future of the Liberal World Order: Internationalism after America. *Foreign Affairs* 90(3):56–69.

Israel, J. 2011. *Democratic Enlightenment: Philosophy, Revolution and Human Rights 1750–1790.* Oxford: Oxford Uniiversity Press.

Johnstone, G., ed. 2003. *A Restorative Justice Reader: Texts, Sources, and Content.* Devon, UK: Willan.

Julius, A. J. 2006. Nagel's Atlas. *Philosophy and Public Affairs* 34:176–92.

Kant, I. 1996. *Practical Philosophy.* Trans. M. J. Gregor. Cambridge, UK: Cambridge University Press.

———. 2005. *Notes and Fragments.* Ed. Paul Guyer. Cambridge, UK: Cambridge University Press.

Katz, C. J. 2003. Thomas Jefferson's Liberal Anrticapitalism. *American Journal of Politics* 47:1–17.

Kelly, E. 2009. Criminal Justice without Retribution. *Journal of Philosophy* 106:440–62.

Keohane, R. O. 1984. *After Hegemony: Cooperation and Discord in the World Political Economy.* Princeton: Princeton University Press.

Kingsbury, B., N. Krisch, and R. Stewart. 2005. The Emergence of Global Administrative Law. *Law and Contemporary Problems* 68:15–61.

Knox, J. H. 2011. Ruggie's Rules: Applying Human Rights Rules to Corporations. *SSRN:* http://ssrn.com/abstract=1916664.

Kramer, M. H. 2003. *The Quality of Freedom.* Oxford: Oxford University Press.

Kukathas, C., and P. Pettit. 1990. *Rawls: A Theory of Justice and Its Critics.* Cambridge, UK: Polity Press; Stanford: Stanford University Press.

Kymlicka, W. 1995. *Multicultural Citizenship.* Oxford: Oxford University Press.

———. 2002. *Contemporary Political Philosophy.* Oxford: Oxford University Press.

Laborde, C. 2008. *Critical Republicanism: The Hijab Controversy and Political Philosophy.* Oxford: Oxford University Press.

———. 2013. Republicanism. In *The Oxford Handbook of Political Ideologies.* Ed. M. Freeden, L. T. Sargent, and M. Stears. Oxford: Oxford University Press.

Laborde, C., and J. Maynor, eds. 2007. *Republicanism and Political Theory.* Oxford: Blackwell.

Laborde, C., and M. Ronzoni. 2012. What Is a Free State? A Republican Account of Sovereignty and International Justice. London: University College, London, Dept of Politics.

Lacey, N. 2008. *The Prisoners' Dilemma: Political Economy and Punishment in Contemporary Democracies.* Cambridge, UK: Cambridge University Press.

Languet, H. 1994. *Vindiciae, Contra Tyrannos.* Cambridge, UK: Cambridge University Press.

Larmore, C. 2001. A Critique of Philip Pettit's Republicanism. *Philosophical Issues* 11:229–43.

Lilburne, J. 1646. *The Legal Fundamental Liberties of the People of England, asserted, revived, and vindicated.* London.

Lind, J. 1776. *Three Letters to Dr Price.* London: T. Payne.

List, C. 2004. The Impossibility of a Paretian Republican? Some Comments on Pettit and Sen. *Economics and Philosophy* 20:1–23.

———. 2006. Republican Freedom and the Rule of Law. *Politics, Philosophy and Economics* 5:201–20.

List, C., and P. Pettit. 2011. *Group Agency: The Possibility, Design and Status of Corporate Agents.* Oxford: Oxford University Press.

———. 2012. Symposium on Group Agency: Replies to Gaus, Cariani, Sylvan, and Briggs. *Episteme* 9:293–309.

Locke, J. 1960. *Two Treatises of Government.* Cambridge, UK: Cambridge University Press.

Long, D. C. 1977. *Bentham on Liberty.* Toronto: University of Toronto Press.

Lovett, F. 2010. *Justice as Non-domination.* Oxford: Oxford University Press.

Lovett, F., and P. Pettit. 2009. Neo-Republicanism: A Normative and Institutional Research Program. *Annual Review of Political Science* 12:18–29.

Lovett, F. N. 2001. Domination: A Preliminary Analysis. *Monist* 84:98–112.

MacDonagh, O. 1958. The 19th-Century Revolution in Government: A Reappraisal. *Historical Journal* 1.

———. 1961. *A Pattern of Government Growth 1800–60.* London: MacGibbon and Kee.

———. 1977. *Early Victorian Government.* London: Weidenfeld and Nicolson.

———. 1980. Pre-transformations: Victorian Britain. In *Law and Social Control.* Ed. E. Kamenka and A. E.-S. Tay. London: Edward Arnold.

MacGilvray, E. 2011. *The Invention of Market Freedom.* Cambridge, UK: Cambridge University Press.

Machiavelli, Niccolò. 1965. *The Complete Works and Others.* Durham, NC: Duke University Press.

Mansbrige, J. 2009. A "Selection Model" of Political Representation. *Journal of Political Philosophy* 17:369–98.

Marti, J. L., and P. Pettit. 2010. *A Political Philosophy in Public Life: Civic Republicanism in Zapatero's Spain.* Princeton: Princeton University Press.

Maynor, J. 2003. *Republicanism in the Modern World.* Cambridge, UK: Polity Press.

McBride, C. 2013. *Recognition.* Cambridge, UK: Polity Press.

McCormick, J. P. 2011. *Machiavellian Democracy.* Cambridge, UK: Cambridge University Press.

Mill, J. S. 2001. *On Liberty.* Kitchener, Ontario: Batoche Books.

———. 2010. *Principles of Political Economy.* Oxford: Oxford University Press.

Milton, J. 1953–82. *Complete Prose Works of John Milton.* 8 vols. New Haven: Yale University Press.

Morris, I. 2010. *Why the West Rules—For Now: The Patterns of History, and What They Reveal about the Future.* New York: Farrar, Straus and Giroux.

Murphy, L., and T. Nagel. 2004. *The Myth of Ownership.* New York: Oxford University Press.

Nagel, T. 1987. Moral Conflict and Political Legitimacy. *Philosophy and Public Affairs* 16:215–40.

———. 1991. *Equality and Partiality.* Oxford: Oxford University Press.

———. 2005. The Problem of Global Justice. *Philosophy and Public Affairs* 33:113–47.

Niederberger, A., and P. Schink, eds. 2013. *Republican Democracy: Liberty, Law and Politics.* Edinburgh: Edinburgh University Press.

Nozick, R. 1974. *Anarchy, State, and Utopia.* Oxford: Blackwell.

Nussbaum, M. 2006. *Frontiers of Justice.* Cambridge, MA: Harvard University Press.

Nye, J. 2004. *Soft Power: The Means to Success in World Politics.* New York: Perseus Books, Public Affairs.

O'Neill, M. 2008. What Should Egalitarians Believe? *Philosophy and Public Affairs* 36:119–56.

Ober, J. 2008. The Original Meaning of "Democracy." *Constellations* 15:3-9.

Olsaretti, S. 2004. *Liberty, Desert and the Market.* Cambridge, UK: Cambridge University Press.

Paley, W. 2002. *The Principles of Moral and Political Philosophy.* Indianapolis: Liberty Fund.

Pettit, P. 1993. A Definition of Physicalism. *Analysis* 53:213–23.

———. 1996. Freedom and Antipower. *Ethics* 106:576–604.

———. 1997a. Republican Theory and Criminal Punishment. *Utilitas* 9:59–79.

———. 1997b. *Republicanism: A Theory of Freedom and Government.* Oxford: Oxford University Press.

———. 2001a. Capability and Freedom: A Defence of Sen. *Economics and Philosophy* 17:1–20.

———. 2001b. The Capacity to Have Done Otherwise. In *Relating to Responsibility: Essays in Honour of Tony Honore on His 80th Birthday.* Ed. P. Cane and J. Gardner. Oxford: Hart. Reprinted in P. Pettit. *Rules, Reasons, and Norms.* Oxford: Oxford University Press, 2002.

———. 2001c. *A Theory of Freedom: From the Psychology to the Politics of Agency.* Cambridge, UK: Polity Press; New York: Oxford University Press.

———. 2002a. Is Criminal Justice Politically Feasible? *Buffalo Criminal Law Review*, special issue ed. Pablo de Greiff, 5(2):427–50.

———. 2002b. Keeping Republican Freedom Simple: On a Difference with Quentin Skinner. *Political Theory* 30:339–56.

———. 2003. Deliberative Democracy, the Discursive Dilemma, and Republican Theory. In *Philosophy, Politics and Society, Vol. 7: Debating Deliberative Democracy.* Ed. J. Fishkin and P. Laslett. Cambridge, UK: Cambridge University Press: 138–62.

———. 2006. Democracy, National and International. *Monist* 89:301–24.

———. 2008a. *Made with Words: Hobbes on Language, Mind and Politics.* Princeton: Princeton University Press.

———. 2008b. Value-mistaken and Virtue-mistaken Norms. In *Political Legitimization without Morality?* Ed. J. Kuehnelt. New York: Springer.

———. 2009. Varieties of Public Representation. In *Representation and Popular Rule*. Ed. Ian Shapiro, Susan Stokes, and E. J.Wood. Cambridge, UK: Cambridge University Press.

———. 2010a. Legitimate International Institutions: A Neorepublican Perspective. In *The Philosophy of Intenational Law*. Ed. J. Tasioulas and S. Besson. Oxford: Oxford University Press.

———. 2010b. Representation, Responsive and Indicative. *Constellations* 3:426–34.

———. 2010c. A Republican Law of Peoples. *European Journal of Political Theory*, special issue "Republicanism and International Relations," 9:70–94.

———. 2011. The Instability of Freedom as Non-Interference: The Case of Isaiah Berlin. *Ethics* 121:693–716.

———. 2012a. Freedom in Hobbes's Ontology and Semantics: A Comment on Quentin Skinner. *Journal of the History of Ideas* 73:111–26.

———. 2012b. The Inescapability of Consequentialism. In *Luck, Value and Commitment: Themes from the Ethics of Bernard Williams*. Ed. U. Heuer and G. Lang. Oxford: Oxford University Press.

———. 2012c. *On the People's Terms: A Republican Theory and Model of Democracy*. Cambridge, UK: Cambridge University Press.

———. 2013a. Reflections on the Occupy Movements. In *Up the Republic*. Ed. F. O'Toole. London: Faber.

———. 2013b. Two Republican Traditions. In *Republican Democracy: Liberty, Law and Politics*. Ed. A. Niederberger and P. Schink. Edinburgh: Edinburgh University Press.

———. 2014a. Criminalization in Republican Theory. In *Criminalization*. Ed. R. A. Duff, Lindsay Farmer, S. E. Marshall, M. Renzo, and V. Tadros. Oxford: Oxford University Press.

———. 2014b. Meritocratic Representation. In *The East Asian Challenge for Democracy: Political Meritocracy in Comparative Perspective*. Ed. D. A. Bell and C. Li. Cambridge, UK: Cambridge University Press.

———. 2015. *The Robust Demands of Doing Good: An Ethics of Attachment, Virtue and Respect*. Oxford: Oxford University Press.

Pettit, P., and M. Smith. 1996. Freedom in Belief and Desire. *Journal of Philosophy* 93:429–49. Reprinted in F. Jackson, P. Pettit, and M. Smith. *Mind, Morality and Explanation* Oxford: Oxford University Press, 2004.

Pinker, S. 2011. *The Better Angels of our Nature: Why Violence Has Declined*. New York: Viking Penguin.

Pocock, J. 1975. *The Machiavellian Moment: Florentine Political Theory and the Atlantic Republican Tradition.* Princeton: Princeton University Press.

Pogge, T. 1990. *Realizing Rawls.* Ithaca, NY: Cornell University Press.

———. 1993. An Egalitarian Law of Peoples. *Philosophy and Public Affairs* 23:195–224.

Price, R. 1991. *Political Writings.* Cambridge, UK: Cambridge University Press.

Priestley, J. 1993. *Political Writings.* Cambridge, UK: Cambridge University Press.

Raventos, D. 2007. *Basic Income: The Material Conditions of Freedom.* London: Pluto Press.

Rawls, J. 1971. *A Theory of Justice.* Oxford: Oxford University Press.

———. 1993. *Political Liberalism.* New York: Columbia University Press.

———. 1999. *The Law of Peoples.* Cambridge, MA: Harvard University Press.

———. 2001. *Justice as Fairness: A Restatement.* Cambridge, MA: Harvard University Press.

Raz, J. 1986. *The Morality of Freedom.* Oxford: Oxford University Press.

Richardson, H. 2002. *Democratic Autonomy.* New York: Oxford University Press.

Riker, W. 1982. *Liberalism against Populism.* San Francisco: Freeman.

Ripstein, A. 2009. *Force and Freedom: Kant's Legal and Political Philosophy.* Cambridge, MA: Harvard University Press.

Robbins, C. 1959. *The Eighteenth-Century Commonwealthman.* Cambridge, MA: Harvard University Press.

Rousseau, J.-J. 1997. *Rousseau: "The Social Contract" and Other Later Political Writings.* Trans. Victor Gourevitch. Cambridge, UK: Cambridge University Press.

Sandel, M. 1996. *Democracy's Discontent: America in Search of a Public Philosophy.* Cambridge, MA: Harvard Universty Press.

Sanyal, S. 2012. A Defence of Democratic Egalitarianism. *Journal of Philosophy* 109:415–34.

Scanlon, T. M. 1998. *What We Owe to Each Other.* Cambridge, MA: Harvard University Press.

Scheffler, S. 2005. Choice, Circumstance and the Value of Equality. *Politics, Philosophy and Economics* 4:5–28.

Schmidtz, D., and J. Brennan. 2010. *A Brief History of Liberty.* Oxford: Wiley Blackwell.

Schumpeter, J. A. 1984. *Capitalism, Socialism and Democracy.* New York: Harper Torchbooks.

Sen, A. 1985. *Commodities and Capabilities.* Amsterdam: North-Holland.

Shapiro, I. 2003. *The State of Democratic Theory.* Princeton: Princeton University Press.

Shapiro, S. 2011. *Legality.* Cambridge, MA: Harvard University Press.

Sharp, A., ed. 1998. *The English Levellers.* Cambridge, UK: Cambridge University Press.

Shiffrin, S. 2000. Paternalism, Unconscionability Doctrine, and Accommodation. *Philosophy and Public Affairs* 29:205–50.

Sidney, A. 1990. *Discourses Concerning Government.* Indianapolis: Liberty Classics.

Simmons, A. J. 1976. Tacit Consent and Political Obligation. *Philosophy and Public Affairs* 5(3):274–291.

———. 1979. *Moral Principles and Political Obligations.* Princeton: Princeton University Press.

———. 1999. Justification and Legitimacy. *Ethics* 109:739–71.

Sintomer, Y. 2007. *Le Pouvoir au Peuple: Jurys citoyens, tirage au sort et democratie participative.* Paris: Edition la Decouverte.

Skinner, Q. 1978. *The Foundations of Modern Political Thought.* Cambridge, UK: Cambridge University Press.

———. 1998. *Liberty Before Liberalism.* Cambridge, UK: Cambridge University Press.

———. 2002. *Visions of Politics, Vol. 2: Renaissance Virtues.* Cambridge, UK: Cambridge University Press.

———. 2008. *Hobbes and Republican Liberty.* Cambridge, UK: Cambridge University Press.

———. 2012. On the Liberty of the Ancients and the Moderns: A Reply to My Critics. *Journal of the History of Ideas* 73:127–46.

Slaughter, A.-M. 1997. The Real New World Order. *Foreign Affairs* 76:183–97.

———. 2004. *A New World Order.* Princeton: Princeton University Press.

Slaughter, S. 2005. *Liberty beyond Neo-Liberalism: A Republican Critique of Liberal Government in a Globalising Age.* London: Macmillan Palgrave.

Smith, A. 1976. *An Inquiry into the Nature and Causes of the Wealth of Nations.* Oxford: Oxford University Press.

Sober, E., and D. S. Wilson. 1998. *Unto Others: The Evolution and Psychology of Unselfish Behavior.* Cambridge, MA: Harvard University Press.

Southwood, N. 2014. Democracy as a Modally Demanding Value. *Nous* 48.

Spitz, J.-F. 1995. *La Liberté Politique.* Paris: Presses Universitaires de France.

Steiner, H. 1994. *An Essay on Rights.* Oxford: Blackwell.

Stilz, A. 2009. *Liberal Loyalty: Freedom, Obligation, and the State.* Princeton: Princeton University Press.

Strang, H., and J. Braithwaite, eds. 2000. *Restorative Justive: Philosophy to Practice.* Aldershot, UK: Dartmouth–Ashgate.

Strawson, P. 1962. *Freedom and Resentment and Other Essays.* London: Methuen.

Sugden, R. 1998. The Metric of Opportunity. *Economics and Philosophy* 14:307–37.

Sunstein, C. 2013. *Simpler: The Future of Government.* New York: Simon and Schuster.

Tan, K.-C. 2008. A Defense of Luck Egalitarianism. *Journal of Philosophy* 105:665–90.

Taylor, R. S. 2013. Market Freedom as Antipower. *American Political Science Review* 107:593–602.

Temkin, L. 1996. *Inequality.* Oxford: Oxford University Press.

Thaler, R., and Sunstein, C. 2008. *Nudge: Improving Decisions about Health, Wealth and Happiness.* London: Penguin Books.

Trenchard, J., and T. Gordon. 1971. *Cato's Letters.* New York: Da Capo.

Tuck, R. 2008. *Free Riding.* Cambridge, MA: Harvard University Press.

Tully, J. 2009. *Public Philosophy in a New Key.* 2 vols. Cambridge, UK: Cambridge University Press.

Tyler, T. R. 1990. *Why People Obey the Law.* New Haven: Yale University Press.

Valentini, L. 2011. *Justice in a Globalized World: A Normative Framework.* Oxford: Oxford University Press.

Vallentyne, P. 2007. Distributive Justice. In *A Companion to Contemporary Political Philosophy.* Ed. R. E. Goodin, P. Pettit, and T. Pogge. Oxford: Blackwell.

Vallentyne, P., and H. Steiner, eds. 2000. *The Origins of Left–Libertarianism.* New York: Palgrave.

Van Gelderen, M., and Q. Skinner. 2002. *Republicanism: A Shared European Heritage.* 2 vols. Cambridge, UK: Cambridge University Press.

Van Parijs, P. 1995. *Real Freedom for All.* Oxford: Oxford University Press.

Vermeule, A. 2011. *The System of the Constitution.* New York: Oxford University Press.

Viroli, M. 2002. *Republicanism.* New York: Hill and Wang.

Waldron, J. 1999a. *The Dignity of Legislation*. Cambridge, UK: Cambridge University Press.

———. 1999b. *Law and Disagreement*. Oxford: Oxford University Press.

Walzer, M. 1981. Philosophy and Democracy. *Political Theory* 9: 379–99.

Warren, M. E., and H. Pearse, eds. 2008. *Designing Deliberative Democracy*. Cambridge, UK: Cambridge University Press.

Weinstock, D., and C. Nadeau, eds. 2004. *Republicanism: History, Theory and Practice*. London: Frank Cass.

White, S., and D. Leighton, eds. 2008. *Building a Citizen Society: The Emerging Politics of Republican Democracy*. London: Lawrence and Wishart.

Winch, P. 1963. *The Idea of a Social Science and Its Relation to Philosophy*. London: Routledge.

Wirszubski, C. 1968. *Libertas as a Political Ideal at Rome*. Oxford: Oxford University Press.

Wollstonecraft, M. 1982. *A Vindication of the Rights of Women*. New York: Whitston.

ACKNOWLEDGMENTS

In the preparation of this book I benefitted greatly from the editorial advice of Anthony Appiah, Roby Harrington, and Jake Schindel, and in particular from the detailed, invariably helpful guidance of Brendan Curry. I was helped enormously too by Mitchell Kohles and my copyeditor, Allegra Huston. I am deeply indebted to them all and I am also very grateful to Cecile Laborde for insightful comments provided on an earlier draft, to Owen Pettit for numerous useful suggestions about the text, and to Tori McGeer for conversations on many of the questions it raises. The book draws together strands from my work in political philosophy over the past twenty years, and my long-standing intellectual debts far outrun any acknowledgments I could hope to make here. But I must mention two individuals in particular, Quentin Skinner and John Braithwaite. Quentin did the historical groundwork that reopened the republican way of thinking for our generation, as well as being a major contributor in his own right to republican political theory, and has been a source of generous support and encouragement over the years. I worked with John in the early 1990s on the republican theory of criminal justice, and it was collaborating with him that first convinced me of the potential of the republican approach. He has established the relevance of republican theory across a wide spectrum, ranging from restorative justice to global regulation to how best to achieve peace in unsettled communities, and has been a constant stimulus in my own thinking. Intellectual community is as important as personal influence, of course, and I cannot conclude without recording my debt and gratitude to colleagues and students at Princeton University and the Australian National University and to the rich intellectual environment that I found, and continue to find, in each institution.

INDEX

Page numbers beginning with 211 refer to endnotes.